Isobel
Kuhn

Lois Hoadley Dick

D1387419

HIGHLAND BOOKS

ISBN: 0 946616 51 5

Printed in Great Britain for
HIGHLAND BOOKS
Broadway House, The Broadway,
Crowborough, East Sussex, TN6 1BY
by Richard Clay Ltd., Bungay, Suffolk

THANK YOU

Elaine Hook of Hawthorne Bible House for being willing to loan rare books to a perfect stranger;

John Vogel who picked up the books during a blizzard;

Rev. and Mrs. John Allen Yates, chalk artist, for delivering the books;

Mr. Osborne, librarian at Moody Bible Institute, for renewing the overdue books;

and the reference librarians of the Sussex County Library, New Jersey, for always managing to find the most impossible requests.

CONTENTS

"Eager faces, watching, waiting
For the lights along the shore . . ."

"Where are the eager faces? I never once met a heathen who was seeking God." —Isobel Kuhn

"There is none that seeketh after God." —Romans 3:11

But altars and temples and prayers and ceremonies and religion fill the land! *"They sacrifice to devils, and not to God."* —1 Corinthians 10:20

"The human race is rotten fruit." —Ancient Greek translation of the word "unprofitable" in Romans 3:12

"The demons . . . believe . . ." —James 2:19

"Devils, working miracles . . ." —Revelation 16:14

Animism: *The belief that everything in nature is animated by living spirits and possesses vitality; i.e., rivers, trees, stones, stars, water, animals, plants, lightning, fire, etc., the spirits necessarily evil because man created them in his own image. And behind them, mighty beings who perpetrate the deceit and crave the worship.*

"He shall speak peace unto the heathen." —Zechariah 9:10

I.

"THE HEATHEN ARE HAPPY!"

The little boy screamed, convulsing with fear as his family stood around the small plank bed looking accusingly at one another.

"Why did you tell him about the *hini*, the ancestral ghost?"

"Well, he saw me decorating the shelf with shreds of red and white paper and an offering of wine, and he asked—"

"You said it would get me!" wailed the child. "You said after Old Two died, her ghost would follow me if I went down the trail!"

"You shouldn't talk about death to a five-year-old," the mother cautioned pulling her son onto her lap.

"But we must all die," the oldest son explained shivering, though the day was hot and sticky. "Old Two's husband announced her spirit name to the ancestors so they would take her quickly away."

"Stop talking about death," the father said in a low tone, but the child heard and wept hysterically. "I won't die! I don't want to die!" he shrieked as he rolled over and pounded his fists on the hard bed. It was days before he calmed down and years before he could pass a wayside grave without a cold shudder flitting up his spine.

"The heathen are happy! Why bother them?"

Up the sides of the Salween River Canyon, rising to 15,000 feet, higher than the Swiss Alps, hemmed in by snow-clad mountains, isolated by dark chasms and haunted ravines, lived the Lisu people.

For centuries, no one knew they were there. The world had never heard of the Lisu Tribe, aborigines of China, pushed out of the country and up the sides of the rocky gorges. Savage, almost too lazy to till the ground, they lurked behind trees and in caves, waiting for any brave trader who dared cross the ranges over the Mekong River, craving the salt he carried. Filthy—morally and in appearance—they dealt directly with demons who demanded blood, not bothering with idols or images. The Chinese had one word for the Lisu—dirt.

In the southwest corner of Tibet, three rivers run side by side within an area of fifty miles, gashed by mountain ranges. The Salween River flows from East Tibet to the Gulf of Mataban in Burma, 1,750 miles long. In juxtaposition are the Mekong and Yangste, forming the Burma-China frontier. Lisuland is officially in West Yunnan Province, China, in the Salween River Canyon.

Long before any white people arrived, the old chief knew the story of the birth of man, the flood and the scattering of the races. The story, however, became distorted from being handed down by word-of-mouth around campfires, and blue-pencilled by a Villain Editor.

Makwa, a great spirit above, threatened a flood. He told a man and his sister to plant pumpkin seeds, for a rain greater than any of their usual downpours would sweep everyone away. A special pumpkin grew to Cinderella-coach size. Under Makwa's guidance, the man hollowed it out; then he and his sister rode the waves in the pumpkin shell and survived the flood. They married and replenished the earth.

The Lisu had not an atom more of divine truth. They knew of no power but evil power. They feared and appeased evil spirits by degraded family ceremonies, sacrificing animals even to the point of wiping out a herd of pigs or a flock of chickens and facing starvation.

Anthropologists visiting the area in 1868 described little swinging altars suspended from trees, mediums by whose mouths demons gave order, witches who cast real spells. The scholars placed the Lisu spoken language in the Lolo group of the Tibeto-Burman family. The Lisu had no written language.

Misi was the great jungle *nat*, or spirit. *Mina* was the earth *nat*; *Muhu*, the lightning demon; *Mihi*, the spirit of the wind; *Chyi*, a demon with healing power.

Demons, though terrifying, could be fooled and so a son would be named Cow-dung. Maybe the evil ones would not notice he was human.

The Lisu loved to sing and dance to the music of native guitar and bamboo Jew's harp. Boys and girls and young people locked fingers together and swayed back and forth in a circle around the fire. Soon arms were around shoulders and the dance whirled faster and faster in wild, weird steps around a golden-blue campfire. A dub-dub-dub drum sound paced their rhythm.

The fiery sunset died, the half-moon rose and still they danced.

One of the dancers, eighteen-year-old Sister Seven, had been forced to marry a cruel opium sot who often beat her. Flushed and warmed by wine, she turned the drench of her eyes upon her twenty-year-old partner in the dance. His eyes burned into hers. Clinging together they dropped out of the circle and disappeared.

Much later that night, she stepped noiselessly into her bamboo hut and murdered her husband as he slept. Together, she and her lover ran away, but tribal justice overtook her.

There were no words in the Lisu tongue such as forgive, mercy, compassion, repent, conscience, or justice. There were, however, hundreds of words describing the best way to skin alive a human being. Sister Seven was skinned alive, beginning with her face. By the time the men reached her waistline, she was still alive and they could see her beating heart.

"The heathen are happy! Why try to change them?"

Malaria, cancer, smallpox and dozens of undiagnosed plagues fell upon the tribespeople. Germs, hygiene, medicine and nutrition were only words—not even included in their language. The demons brought the plague! Make a sacrifice! So the drums throbbed again in eerie monotony.

Two village women hopping from foot to foot, calling to the evil spirits. "Come down! Come down!" Soon every shack in the village joined in the cry.

In one shanty—merely four stakes planted in the ground, bleached bamboo walls, branch roof—an only child lay dying of blood poisoning. The devoted mother had smeared fresh manure over the wound and denied the child food and water at a witch's command.

Suddenly the two dancing women were possessed by demons and slumped unconscious to the ground while a man's voice shouted through their mouths: "Sacrifice the ox for the child!"

Possession fell upon everyone in the village. When they awoke, they remembered.

"We can't plow without the ox," the father argued.

"But we can't lose our only little one!" wept the broken-hearted mother.

And so the ox was slaughtered and the blood poured out on the ground as a sacrifice to the demon. The child died.

"The heathen are happy! Let them alone!"

In another village it was time to play "Hang the demons" and rid the homes of their presence. The exorcist was called in, an old man completely given over to the Evil One. The family demon shelf opposite the door was lit up by a crude tin-can lamp. Fear hung in the air—it could be felt!

The exorcist chanted incantations, hopped in a circle swinging a weapon, then fell to the floor and rolled himself up in a newly woven cloth. Deep in a trance, his voice warbled to a high pitch, reminiscent of graveyards and flying bats and chills down the spine. But it was no game they were playing.

Each family member lit a small lamp and searched every crack and corner of the house, lifting the bed mats, snooping into pots and pans, behind jars. They found nothing, so were satisfied the demons were gone for the time being. But they were still present.

A field explorer for *National Geographic* magazine, traveling those slopes in the 1930s, pitched a tent each night and slept with two pistols under his pillow. Exactly at 4:00 a.m. he saw *them*. He saw the demons and sprayed them with bullets, then sat hunched over and shaking in his sleeping bag until the sun rose. No one would travel with him for fear of being shot. The man was literally haunted, but his articles to the world on animism and the native never gave a hint of it.

> Lord, in the darkness I wander,
> Where is the lamp? Is there no lamp?
> Nothing know I, but I wonder,
> Is there no lamp? Where is the lamp?
> Lord, in the vastness I wander,
> Where is the way? Is there no way?
> How may I reach Thee, I wonder.
> Is there no way? Where is the way?

Are the heathen happy?

"Once faith was like a flood . . ." —Matthew Arnold

"Faith must have adequate evidence, else it is mere superstition." —A. A. Hodge, theologian

"Faith is . . . evidence . . ." —Hebrews 11:1

"Faith in order, which is the basis of science, cannot reasonably be separated from faith in an Ordainer, which is the basis of religion." —Asa Gray, botanist

"There can be no real conflict between science and the Bible— between nature and the Scriptures—the two books of the Great Author. Both are revelations made by Him to man." —James Dana, geologist

"Science should lead us to think of Him who wrought all those mysteries. Christ's works do continually glorify Him." —Michael Faraday, master physicist

"All human discoveries seem to be made only for the purpose of confirming more and more strongly the truths that come from on high and are contained in the Sacred Writings." —Sir John Herschel, astronomer

II.

BELLE WAS HER NAME

1901–1922

"Belle" was her nickname and "belle" described her, from the top of her daringly bobbed brown hair to her slipper-clad feet which could dance all night and beg for more.

The Roaring Twenties spawned a dance fever. The Charleston, Black Bottom and Heebie-Jeebies were danced by flappers and society matrons alike all over America. Dance halls opened by the thousands. Hotels and bars added dance floors. Nightclubs pulsated night after night to the beat of Dixieland and blues. Working women and female students, liberated by the upsetting values of the war years, cut loose and lived a frivolous life of fun.

Belle topped them all. She was cute and petite, dainty as a teaspoon with a turned up nose and lively mischievous eyes. A little actress, specializing in comic parts, she toured with the University Players Club. And how she could dance! Dancing was her life.

She was born Isobel Selina Miller, on December 17, 1901, in Toronto, Canada. Brother Murray was almost three years older. Belle's parents were Christians, pillars and workers in a Presbyterian church. Her father was a lay

preacher at a rescue mission, her mother, Alice, played the
piano, and the two children sang.

"Such a good girl!" people described Belle. And she *was*
good, with the human goodness that came through faithfully
attending Sunday school and church, a few verses of Bible
reading each morning, a prayer said at night. She even
signed a temperance pledge, promising never to touch liquor, and attended prayer meetings of the China Inland Mission. However, Belle's emotions at times would flare high,
and temper tantrums, rebellion, tears and threats to "run
away" were common.

Belle's father, Sam, specialized in electric therapeutics
and helped the Victor Electric Company build its first X-
ray machine. Constantly on the move, he opened agencies
in Pittsburgh, Philadelphia, Cleveland, St. Louis and other
places all over the United States and Canada. Usually he
left his family behind when he traveled, but never failed to
bring back gifts, surprises and souvenirs. He made good
money as a salesman, but he also enjoyed spending money.
His generous nature opened his wallet to almost anyone
who asked for a loan. Belle learned early in life to pray for
her daily bread.

When she was eleven years old, the family moved to
Vancouver, British Columbia, situated at the feet of the Ca-
nadian Rockies. Overlooking a beautiful harbor, Vancouver
provided everything Belle could want with its water to play
in, mountains to climb, and hymn sings around a campfire
at night.

In high school Belle received the Governor General's
medal for scholastic ability, ranking number one in British
Columbia. When her mother insisted she study speech ("to
learn to express yourself nicely") and dancing ("so you will
move gracefully in society"), Belle couldn't have been more
cooperative. In fact, she threw herself into those two activ-
ities so thoroughly that Mother became alarmed.

"I don't approve of the late hours, night after night," she
protested. "I don't like you away from home almost every

weekend with the Players Club. You're involved with a pretty godless crowd now, Belle."

"What difference does it make, if I keep my grades high?" Belle pouted. She'd tasted the world's pleasures. Popularity was a heady wine. She knew she was riding the crest of the wave, right up there on top.

One day while cleaning out her bureau drawers, she found a childhood autograph book. Her grandmother's spidery, faded blue handwriting was on the first page:

> A noble life is not a blaze
> Of sudden glory won.
> But just an adding up of days
> In which good work is done.

"How dull," she thought. *"I'll take the blaze of glory."*

The campus of the University of British Columbia was an ideal setting for a girl who wanted to shine. Belle attracted friends like a magnet pulls pins, and won honors, all the while staying on top scholastically, dancing and acting with the drama group. Before she entered the university, her dad had carefully coached her in all the arguments against modernism, but without a direct confrontation with a living Savior she was standing in her own strength.

"Every man must fall for himself, that he may have his own measure of self-revelation." The attack came not with a denunciation of Christianity but with a quiet, almost kindly rebuke that somehow was worse. "You just believe because Mama and Papa told you to."

The speaker was Dr. Sedgewick, head of the English department where Belle studied Language and Literature. "For example," he went on, "does anyone here still believe the Genesis account of creation? Or in heaven and hell?"

Out of one hundred students, Belle's hand lifted bravely. She glanced around, embarrassed. Only one other hand was raised. Dr. Sedgewick was not insulting nor did he wish to humiliate anyone. Just a patronizing smile and a teasing remark. But on the short walk home from his class, Belle became an agnostic. Not an atheist, for she had seen answers to prayer. Or *were* they really answers? Psychology taught that mind could influence matter. Were answers to prayer only coincidence? Didn't people sometimes answer their own prayers?

"From now on I will believe nothing that I have not proven by experience," she decided. "I will figure things out for myself, not lean on my parents."

There was no plunging into a wild life of open sin, no drastic outward change, just subtle changes seen by her family. First, "drop church," she told herself. "Why waste my time if there is no God, or if we can't find Him? If the Bible is unscientific and outdated, why get up early to force myself through a chapter? Why pray when I can't be sure He's there?"

So Belle slept later each morning and used Sundays to catch up on sleep after dancing the nights away. On campus she was still tagged as a "good Christian girl." But she knew the emptiness of her own heart.

In the second year at the university she held the highest position to which a female student could be elected: secretary of the Student Council. It was then that Ben stepped into her life. A veteran of World War I, over six feet tall, a nominal Baptist, a star athlete, he was out to get the best from life. And he wanted Belle.

They were secretly engaged for two years. When Belle was a senior, her shaky world caved in. Her best friend, Cora, took her aside and said, "You're the only one who doesn't know. Ben has been carrying on with other women behind your back."

"I'll never believe that!" Belle's pride retorted. "I'd have to hear him say it." But her heart shriveled within her, for lately she had sensed the change. He just took her for granted. He cancelled dates, and sometimes never showed up.

Then one day seeing him entering the school gates, Belle knew she must confront him. "Ben!" she called. Slowly Ben stopped and turned around and grinned as he saw Belle running up toward him.

Swallowing the hard lump in her throat and forcing a cheery smile, she proceeded.

"Ben, someone said they saw you one night with Reba at the Midnight Club. The night you told me you were in bed with a sore throat." Batting her eyes and putting a slight pout on her face, she waited for him to deny it.

As with a child, he looked down at her, provoked, but very patient. "Don't be so naive, Belle. Do you think that even after we're married, I'm going to be tied to only one woman?"

Her heart felt as though it had been wrenched from her. "Well," she said, hardly able to speak, "it's all over for us then." Without another word, she turned and walked briskly away. All his love talk, a sieve of promises. Light-headed, she couldn't think clearly. His face flashed before her. His lower lip curled when he said it—how could he? Her cheeks flared with color. The shame of it! All the campus discussing her!

At night when others slept, she twisted and tossed and wept The heavy strokes of her heart were like the hammer falling on the anvil. The clock struck the hours and halves, all night long, night after night, dreams and hopes all cankered.

Days, she fought her way through a busy schedule—pushing, driving herself into exhaustion. Nights, she returned like a worn bird to her nest unable to sleep. Nerve-wracking days continued. Exams. And her mother—wringing her hands and crying over and over, "He's such a fine young man, a Baptist, I don't understand why you've broken up!"

Late one night her father tapped at her door, quietly entered, knelt by her bed and prayed for her. Belle sighed. "Thanks for caring, Dad, but what good will that do? Prayer goes only as high as the ceiling."

More hopeless, unhappy days followed. Unable to eat she lost weight. The effort to keep smiling and chattering gaily was almost more than she could bear. Life was all pain

18 *Isobel Kuhn*

and heartache. Why endure more?

Only nineteen, yet she felt aged. During the week of Christmas, she realized she hadn't had a good night's sleep in weeks. Sitting on her bed one night, swaying on the edge of a breakdown, she listened to her thoughts . . . or was it the voice of another, an evil one who wanted her life ended?

In the medicine cabinet . . . the bottle labeled poison . . . drink it . . . why suffer? After death comes nothing . . . a long sleep . . . forever.

In the hall she soundlessly turned the big glass knob of the bathroom door, then heard her father groan in his sleep. She hesitated. If she killed herself, her dad would live out his days wondering if she were in hell. Of course there is no such place, she told herself, but can I do that to Daddy? Some Christmas present! She could see the headlines: CO-ED KILLS SELF! HONOR STUDENT VOTED "MOST POPULAR" DIES BY OWN HAND!

She couldn't. Tiptoeing back to her room Belle sat down again, more miserable than she had ever been in her life. She didn't want to live. She didn't care to die.

No one was looking now. No one was there to laugh. Lifting her hands up to heaven, she cried, "God . . . if You are there, prove yourself to me. Give me peace now at this terrible time. I will give You my life . . . do anything . . . go anywhere . . ."

Silently then she curled up in the blankets and immediately fell into a sound sleep. The next morning a shimmer-shine of sunlight woke her. Surprised, she sat up and realized she had slept like a baby!

She had made a "bargain"—and the other side kept His part! *No need to tell anyone*, she thought. *After all, it still could be just coincidence.*

"Not likely," a voice inside nudged. "You haven't slept like that since you broke with Ben."

Belle didn't talk about her experience, didn't take up church-going again, yet people noticed a difference in her. She seemed more peaceful!

As the days passed by she thought a lot about how she could continue her part of the "bargain." Could she ask for more things and get answers? Her mind flashed back to 1921. She had been a delegate from the YWCA to a Christian convention. She recalled the words of a man's testimony. When he was a prisoner of war in Germany, he was given a Bible. She saw again his radiant face as he said, "I found God through reading His Word." Was that the way?

Her hand reached up to the top bookshelf and pulled down the dusty Bible left unopened since her high school days. The Old Testament, of course, had been proven all wrong, she reasoned, but maybe somewhere in the Gospels she could find God. She began to pray for things important to her at the time: dates, invitations to the best parties, the biggest ball games. And she got them.

Once a year her friend Jill threw a very special party and this year it was in her brand new home with extra rooms especially for dancing. Belle was dancing with Les at the party when the front door flew open and Ben, his arm around Reba, crashed the party. A garnet flush over her cheeks, Belle trembled so much she staggered against her partner, tripped and almost fell flat. Breaking away from Les, she ran upstairs to the bathroom, afraid she was going to be sick.

"Oh, God, if You are there," she prayed again, "give me p—" Before she could even pronounce the word, a warm peace swept through her, she stopped shaking, and stood poised and in control. God had answered again, for she had been on the verge of hysterics. Help had come completely from outside herself.

Calmly, she descended the staircase like a queen. Throughout the evening, she smiled graciously, enjoyed the supper, and even danced with Ben.

Later, alone, the thrilling thought seeped into her being: "God is there . . . and He is trying to get in touch with me!"

Her mother was the one who began the campaign. "Belle, dear, will you go with me to hear a Professor Ellis speak? It's not church, just a Bible class. Can't you go just to please me? I hate to go alone."

Oh, why not? Belle sighed. She owed her mother a favor. After meeting Professor Ellis, one thought came to Belle's mind: "He has found God!" Discovering an eager desire to listen to this kind, scholarly, cultured gentleman, she returned week after week to his Bible study, and the Holy Spirit, who had been seeking *her*, used the Word of God to open her soul and let light pour in. She was born again. She now believed what she had proven by experience.

Growth was slow, as growth usually is, but God had planted signposts along Belle's way to point her in the right direction.

In May 1922, Belle was graduated from the University of British Columbia and needed only five months' training in Normal School to earn her teaching certificate. Always a lover of good literature and classics, her desire was to teach English on a college level and perhaps advance to being a Dean of Women. Nine months later, she began teaching third graders at the Cecil Rhodes School in Vancouver, living in a boardinghouse, finally out in the world on her own.

Belle wanted to continue her "bargain" with God, and asked Him to wake her at 2:00 a.m. each morning, when it was quiet. Always a deep sleeper, it was a miracle to her when she was awakened at the exact time day after day and spent a quiet hour studying her Bible and praying. She was finding a person-to-person friendship with a living Lord.

Life in the classroom, however, wasn't as satisfying as she had hoped. Eight-year-old arithmetic, spelling and exercises proved to be dull. And the adorable little eight-year-old students could find more ways to misbehave faster than the teacher could find ways to correct them.

"Maybe I need more training," she thought, after an especially harrowing day when the cherubs decided to open all the windows and walk around the second-story ledge when she left the room for a few minutes. The day when

Stevie and Ray and Billie mixed sawdust and paste to make
papier mâché and their hands hardened in the mixture and
had to be sawed out. The day Lillie threw up on Belle's desk
and Marily gashed her arm with a razor.

Over the Easter holidays Belle signed up for a teachers'
convention in Seattle. She wrote to Don, an old boyfriend,
whose mother offered their home for the week. At the same
time her father sent her a wire: "Have arranged for you to
stay at Whipples' in Seattle."

"Nuts! What a mean thing to do! Now all my fun will be
spoiled!" She remembered the Whipples as very religious
people. There was no time to reply to her father. She had
to catch a ship.

Don met her in Seattle and they dined and danced. At
a perfectly awful hour that night Belle rang Whipples' door-
bell and prepared herself for a lecture and a few pointed
references to her soul.

Mrs. Otis Whipple, a stout bubbly everybody's mother
type, laughed, hugged Belle and showed her to her room.
Not a scolding nor a mention of religion Belle. relaxed. On
Sunday morning she even bent to custom and attended
church and later on that day looked up an old friend, Mamie.

Taking one look at Belle's discontented face, Mamie
said, "Are you happy teaching school?"

Tearfully Belle sighed and exploded. "No! I hate it! I
really want to teach high school in the city, but I'm only
twenty-one. I need experience. I thought teaching would
be my life's work; now I'm all mixed up."

"I know the perfect solution," Mamie said smoothly.
"You need to see a phrenologist."

"A what?"

"You know, have your head read. He feels the lumps and
bumps and looks at the size of your nose and chin and tells
your destiny. And guess what! Dr. X, noted phrenologist,
is coming here to our house for supper tonight. His service
is very expensive, but I'm sure he wouldn't charge a dinner

guest. You must stay the evening!"

"Marvelous! But on a Sunday? I'm staying with the Whipples, and they keep the Sabbath very strictly. They'll expect me to be in church again tonight, so let me ask them first. Oh, how wonderful it would be to know what my destiny is!"

Belle hurried back to the Whipples' and put the question bluntly: "Would you mind my going? I haven't been happy in my work."

"Let's talk about it," advised Mrs. Whipple. "Step into Miss McClausland's room; she's a schoolteacher, too. I'll be right back."

It was years later Belle discovered that Mrs. Whipple had run into the kitchen, cornered three teenage girls who were Christians and said, "Pray for Belle. She's facing a crisis!"

Back in the schoolteacher's room, with Mrs. Whipple, Belle began to pour out her troubles and ended by saying, "So would you mind if I went to consult the phrenologist on a Sunday?"

Tenderly and assuringly, Mrs. Whipple only said, "God does have a plan for your life and you can find out from Him."

Belle was taken by surprise. No one had ever told her that. She assumed she must intelligently plan her own life. Later if she ever made mistakes or got into trouble, *then* God would help her.

"His plan will always agree with Scriptures," Mrs. Whipple encouraged. "I have always found His will for my life in His Book."

Belle reached over and pulled Mrs. Whipple's family Bible onto her lap. *God's plan for my life—in that Book?* she thought. *Wonder what it says about phrenology.*

She opened it at random, her finger dropping halfway down the page to Ex. 23:7: "Keep thee far from a false matter."

She was so startled at the instantaneous answer that she

burst into tears. For almost two years she had searched for God, through heartache and confusion, keeping up a brave front, and now she was worn out and ready to try God's way.

She didn't keep the appointment with the phrenologist. She had been shown a better way, and seeking God's will for her life was only the beginning of an adventure that was to carry her clear to the other side of the world and 15,000 feet up the side of a river canyon.

"If we walk in the light, as he is in the light, we have fellowship one with another, and the blood of Jesus Christ his Son cleanseth us from all sin." —1 John 1:7

"What can strip the seeming beauty
From the idols of the earth?
Not a sense of right or duty
But a sight of peerless worth.
'Tis the look that melted Peter,
'Tis the face that Steven saw;
'Tis the heart that wept with Mary
Can alone from idols draw.
Draw and win and fill completely
Till the cup overflows its brim;
What have we to do with idols
Since we've companied with him?"
                                    —J.S. Holden

"Indulgence brings fog." —C.S. Lewis

"Many who are saved are not servants. We yield our disordered time-piece to the watchmaker, our costly gem with its broken setting to the jeweler, our wounded bleeding limb to the hand of the surgeon. Can we do less toward God with the priceless treasure of our life if we would have it meet our highest aspirations?"
—James McConkey

"Truly our fellowship is with the Father." —1 John 1:3

III.

IF WE WALK IN THE LIGHT

1923–1924

Something was wrong. The first love had gone out of her new life in Christ. Racing up the stairs of the boardinghouse to her room late one night after a dance, Belle overslept the next morning, but groped for the Bible by her bed. In a fog, she read a chapter, *tried* to think what it meant, *tried* to get through to the Lord. Maybe that's what was wrong—lately she had *tried* so hard.

Praying was like reciting a poem instead of a heart-to-heart talk. The Word of God tasted so flat.

Dad scolded about her worldly living, her preoccupation with amusement and fun, but Belle remembered Dr. Sedgewick's words: ". . . because Papa and Mama told you to." It worked both ways. She no longer believed "just because she was told" to, but neither would she give up anything simply because Papa and Mama said so.

Dancing is a way to keep in touch with my unsaved friends, she consoled herself. In fact, that very night Mac was taking her out.

In the Ladies' Room, retouching her lipstick, Belle peered into the mirror of the blue ruffled dressing table and

25

over her shoulder she saw Marion! Marion, a Christian who
never danced, who walked close to the Lord. Belle often
envied the contentment she saw on Marion's face.

"Why, Marion! What are you doing at a dance!"

Marion laughed giddily. "Well, it's your fault, Belle! All
through college I was left out of the fun. I've heard you are
a good Christian, and you dance! So I decided to dance!"

Belle left the dressing room and, in a state of shock, let
her partner, Keith, lead her onto the dance floor. Why was
she so shocked? Was it the feeling she had led someone
astray?

Waltzing in Keith's arms, Belle only half-listened to his
chatter, then suddenly heard him end up, ". . . old fogies
who still believe in God."

Belle's heart leaped. Wasn't this a God-given chance to
witness? "I believe in God," she said eagerly. "I've been
investigating Him and I have proof He exists."

Scowling, Keith remarked, "I quit being so gullible after
studying science. What kind of proof are you talking about
anyway?" He swung her sharply around. Her skirt flared
out. Belle almost stepped on his foot, flushed and began to
argue. Their voices grew louder. On and on they danced in
the center of the floor until they heard a burst of laughter
sweep around the edges of the ballroom.

The dance had long ended, the orchestra was silent,
while she and Keith made fools of themselves, quarreling
in public. Keith angrily showed her to a seat and hurried
away, never speaking to her again.

Over the next few days, Belle thought about that inci-
dent, very upset that her "witness" for Christ had made an
enemy. Her friend Mac phoned again to ask her to the Ag-
ricultural Ball in spring. Belle put him off. "That's so far
ahead. Could you call me again in a week or two?"

To escape her uneasiness, Belle turned to an exciting
paperback, a love story, lurid and melodramatic. She read
until 1:00 a.m., then picked up her Bible. Such a dull Book.
Dry as dust. Whatever made her think it was alive? She

tried to pray but again it was a dead-end street. "Guess I'm just tired," she decided.

Later, on her way to work she stopped in a grocery store for cough drops and saw Theresa, one of her eight-year-old pupils, having an ice cream cone, a bottle of soda and a bag of penny candy.

"You won't be hungry for your nice hot lunch if you eat that junk food," rebuked Belle. "You won't be hungry for meat and carrots and pudding."

"Don't like them no more." Theresa alternately licked the cone and sipped the sweet drink.

Belle pocketed the cough drops and walked on. "Lord, what's the matter with You? You seem to have left me. What's the matter with Your Word? It bores me."

And in her mind she saw the child Theresa again, feeding on junk food. "Oh—! Lord, do you mean I'm like that?"

That evening the other boarders in the house asked her to participate in a card gambling. Belle always joined them, but this time she held back. Such a waste of brain energy and what did it profit?

"If you don't want to join us," said one, "why don't you play the piano? You could practice your hymns that way." So almost every night Belle played the piano while the others gambled. That left her free to go to bed on time without offending them.

Still, life was monotonous now that the Lord seemed to have hidden His face. So lonely, she felt like something washed up on a rock and left exposed to the elements. She felt like the bride in Solomon's song: "I sought him and could not find him. I called him, but he gave me no answer."

One night she went to the theater by herself. The movie was a silly, perfectly innocent, mushy love story. Certainly nothing in it was immoral or obscene, but she walked home terribly discontent, yearning for romance and adventure. Again, Bible reading did not satisfy her, for it was only that— reading the Bible. Her prayer was formal and stiff, for it, too, was only that—a prayer.

One evening after supper Belle was alone in her room, a typical furnished room of that day—ugly stolid furniture, dark puce wallpaper, brown lineoleum on the floor. Everything guaranteed not to show the dirt. Dismally she felt the tears come. "Lord, is this all there is to life?" she sobbed. "Only twenty-one and no regular boyfriend, nothing but work and church and praying and Bible study."

Falling into a lumpy, overstuffed chair, she opened the Book at random. "Lord, please speak to me like You used to do."

Her hand dropped down beside John 6:67–68: "Will ye also go away?" And the words following: "Then Simon Peter answered him, Lord, to whom shall we go? Thou hast the words of eternal life."

No threats, nor warnings of punishment, not even scolding, just this: *Would you rather have those things or Me? Do you want to completely belong to the world, do as you please, or have Me? Do you want the friendship of the world or My companionship? Do you want to drift or be anchored? Do you want to spend life or invest it?*

Belle bowed her head and covered her face with her hands. "There is no one nor anything I want but You," she cried.

In that moment, He who inhabits eternity condescended to fill the room with His holy presence. From then on Belle never looked back.

Mac was due to call any day for that dance date, and when the phone rang she thought, *If I say no, I'll lose the only boyfriend I have.* But it was Mrs. Whipple, in town for a day, who called. Within an hour Belle was sitting by her, sharing her problem.

"Have you told Mac you are a Christian?"

Belle shook her head. "That's part of my private life I don't talk about. Look what happened when I told Keith. If people should *ask* me a reason for my faith and hope, that would be a different matter."

Silence hung between them. *Why don't they ask?* Belle's heart cried.

"You're compromising," Mrs. Whipple said kindly. Opening her Bible to 2 Cor. 5:17, she read: "If any man be in Christ, he is a new creature: old things are passed away; behold, all things are become new."

Belle thought: *Certainly the old things in life do not compare to the new fellowship with God.* Mrs. Whipple continued: "Be ye not unequally yoked together with unbelievers. . . . What communion hath light with darkness? . . . Come out from among them, and be ye separate."

If Mother and Dad had ordered me to do it, she thought, *I'd rebel. But Jesus himself is telling me. Haven't I proved by experience that He wants me completely for himself— that He will not share me with the world?* "I'll tell Mac," she concluded. "I wonder what he will think?"

"The Lord will take care of it," Mrs. Whipple assured her.

A few days later Mac called.

"Hi, Belle, have you decided about the Ag Ball?"

"Mac, I am a Christian now . . ." Belle thought her throat would close, it was that dry. "I've decided to give up dancing. I've had some experiences . . . I mean . . . I feel the Lord is asking this of me."

Mac was definitely surprised, but after a pause he said heartily, "Thanks for being honest and not leading me on, Belle. Would you like to go to the baccalaureate service instead?"

Belle was delighted. He hadn't just dumped her, he asked for another date instead!

In no time at all she was back on her schedule of early to bed, awake at 2:00 a.m. for a devotional time. *Devotion*— she looked up the word in the dictionary. "To dedicate, to consecrate, to give over wholly." Nobody had posted a list of "don'ts." Mama and Papa hadn't said it must be so. By hiding His face, the Lord himself had made it plain that He wanted Belle for himself.

To give up a list of things to gain the approval of other

people? That wasn't it at all. To demand others take on her personal convictions in this? Or look down her nose if they didn't? Definitely not. Once back in communion with God, all the lesser things simply lost their appeal. She didn't even miss them.

That was only the beginning of the new Belle. More ugly and offensive were the "hyphenated" sins that must go: self-pity, self-righteousness, self-love, among others.

Mrs. Whipple became a spiritual mother to Belle. She saw Belle as a sincere seeker after God, but a young person still ungrounded in the Word, lacking Christian fellowship. In the summer of 1923, Mrs. Whipple was hostess at The Firs, Bellingham, Washington, a small Bible conference she and her husband had founded, now only in its third year. Funds were low, money for new clothes nonexistent, and her only pair of shoes worn out.

Mrs. Whipple was given five dollars "for a pair of shoes." She held the money thankfully in her hand, but her thoughts went out to Belle. Five dollars would pay for a round-trip boat ticket to bring Belle to the conference. Room and board would be "on the house." Belle would hear the best of Bible teachers.

The letter with the five dollars inside arrived, but Belle had not the least desire to go. She'd signed up for six weeks of summer school.

"I asked for a week off and the Registrar refused," a friend told her. "You can't just take off ten days in the middle of the session; you won't get all your credits."

Belle, a little wiser since her surrender to Christ, asked the Lord to decide. "If you want me to go," she prayed, "let the Registrar agree without reducing my credits."

Her friend tossed her head at Belle's wishful dreaming. "No way," she predicted. "They refused me *seven* days."

Belle approached the Registrar the next morning and explained. The man frowned. "Ten days?" He pretended to be engrossed in the book he was reading, then abruptly said, "All right, Miss Miller. Let us know when you return."

Belle walked out of his office as if in a dream. In truth, her God had power!

At The Firs, Belle fell in love with everything—the piney groves, the other girls and fellows her age, evenings around a crackling fireplace, singing, her own cabin in the woods and roommate Edna.

Edna, a young widowed missionary to China, gave a talk one day on consecration and presented the challenge of missions.

Belle, a comfort-loving homebody by nature, made a decision. If God was calling her, then of course she would go. After all, she had promised that the night God saved her from suicide. "I will give you my life . . . do anything . . . go anywhere." And He kept His part of the "bargain."

After the conference ended, Mrs. Whipple loaned her a book about the life of Hudson Taylor, founder of the China Inland Mission. As Belle read of the Chinese women and their many sorrows, living in darkness with no Light to guide them, she felt a call to China. "How shall they believe? How shall they hear?" haunted her. She knew she had found her destiny—and without the dubious help of a phrenologist.

The following summer she returned with joy to The Firs. The main speaker that year was J. O. Fraser of the China Inland Mission. Belle discovered later he was also a brilliant pianist, an electrical engineer, and an honors graduate from London University.

At first the China Inland Mission sent him to a far corner of West China where Yunnan Province met Burma. He loved the Chinese and ministered faithfully to them. One day while shopping for fresh vegetables, he noticed strangers—not Chinese, not Burmese, not Tibetans. The men wore broad flat turbans almost as big as wagon wheels. The women trimmed their dresses with shells and silver rings. He inquired about them.

"They are earth people—dirt!" spat the shopkeeper. "Ai-yah! Keep away from them. Demons live in them!"

Belle leaned back in her seat in the auditorium that evening and prepared to enjoy Mr. Fraser's talk. In fact, it was told so realistically that she lived through the experiences with him.

"There is no neutral ground in the universe; every square inch, every split second, is claimed by God and counterclaimed by Satan." —C. S. Lewis

"When He says 'go,' we stay at our peril. William Carey might have been the pastor of a little English village, but now he is the Apostle of India." —Charles Cowman

"I used to think that prayer should have the first place and teaching the second. I now feel it would be truer to give prayer the first, second, and third places, and teaching the fourth." —J. O. Fraser

"You are crying to Me to do a big work among the Lisu; I am wanting to do a big work in you." —The Lord

"We must serve God even to the point of suffering." —Dr. J. Hudson Taylor

"Torture, darkness and deep despair,
Reading it all in my easy chair."
                              —Amy Carmichael

"The Order of the Steadfastly Set Face, by whose numbers the world's darkest places are still, as of old, illumined and its arid wastes transformed into gardens of God." —J. Stuart Holden

"There remaineth yet very much land to be possessed." —Joshua 13:1

"The labourers are few." —Luke 10:2

IV.

LISTENING TO FRASER

"Ma-pa chi la-o!" The white man dressed like a Chinese coolie cupped his hands around his mouth and yodelled Lisu words: "The male teacher is arriving!"

Dogs barked, children screamed, and men and women in colorful rags scrambled helter-skelter down the steep descent from a village perched on a rock ledge.

The Christians lined up and passed by in single file, pumping the foreign teacher's hand, giving him gifts of eggs. These people had their own church and even a "prophet's chamber" built on especially for their missionary. The people not only supported themselves by hard work in the field and in the hunt, but even sent Lisu evangelists to unreached tribes. Two hundred Christian families were scattered throughout the canyon.

It was not always so. Fraser, lover of mountains and climbing, lover of solitude and challenge, was the first Christian missionary to pioneer in the Salween River Canyon. In 1911 his dream of staying in a Lisu home came true—for a whole week.

The Koh family of Trinket Mountain was one of seven households in that remote spot. Fraser, with the help of his musical ear, already had a list of four hundred Lisu phrases written down phonetically. He still did not speak Lisu and his Chinese was rather sketchy.

He found the Lisu people affectionate and merry. They put their arms around him as though he were one of the family. In his pigeon-Chinese and with the help of their trade-Chinese, Fraser taught them a hymn and a prayer. Over and over the Koh family sang the hymn, sitting nights around a smokey wood fire, pine chips lying in a heap for use as torches when needed.

After a few nights of singing the only hymn they knew, the family members turned uneasily to look at a dusty shelf at the back of the room. Red paper strips, an incense burner, dry leaves, a bowl of food—the accouterments of demon worship. One day, mother, father and the four sons, without a word from Fraser, pulled down the demon shelf and burned it in the fire.

"We want to worship only the true God and His Son, Jesus," the father managed to make Fraser understand.

Other villages called upon him, villages with names like Water Bowl, Pine Mountain, Turtle Village, Oak Flat, Six Family Hollow, Cold Horse Village, Valley of Ease, Mottled Hill, Cow's Hump.

"I enjoy few things more than tramping over these hills," Fraser said, whether swinging up the mountainside hand over hand or roughriding a horse day after day. Sometimes he dined on roast weasel or a stale egg.

Once he was pressed into being master of ceremonies at the first Christian wedding in southern Lisuland. "No liquor," he stated laying down the law. The jars of whiskey were mixed with pig food and dumped out for the swine.

A Lisu wedding was a noisy affair, with everyone invited, so Fraser did not attempt to hold a typical western ceremony. He asked the bride and groom to pause for prayer before stepping over the threshold of their new home. The bride and her two best friends coyly draped a large rug over their heads out of modesty. Friends began to throw potatoes and other hard root vegetables at each other, but Fraser asked them to stop.

"People can be hurt."

"Oh yes, they are hurt, especially the bride," laughed the Lisu, but they gave in to the white man's eccentricity. When Fraser learned that the vegetable throwing was associated with witchcraft, it was never again used at a Christian wedding.

A few days after the wedding the old father removed his demon shelf, saying, "Jesus is our Savior now." Within hours a knifing pain began in his back and spread all over his body until he was in agony.

"The demons," whispered the family, resorting quickly to all the native remedies for deliverance. But the pain persisted.

Finally, a light broke into the mind of one son. "Why not pray to our God about father?"

After prayer, the father was able to fall asleep and by morning was perfectly well.

By now Fraser was speaking excellent Chinese and Lisu. After one journey up and down the river canyon, he wrote a fourteen-page report: He had discovered three hundred little villages with a total of more than ten thousand Lisu people besides many from the Kachin and Shan tribes. "Souls that are still unreached and for whom no man cares," he said.

"Teach me to pray," begged a female innkeeper who overheard Fraser witnessing to some of her guests. He had time only to teach her a short prayer. The next morning as he was leaving, she tried to retain him. "Tell me again," she pleaded. "After you are gone, there will be no one to teach me, and I do want to remember how to pray to Him."

One day the demon-priest of Cold Horse Village invited Fraser to a sword-ladder festival where he would bathe his hands in fire and climb a ladder of razor-edged swords without harm. "The demons have entered into me and I belong to them," explained the priest.

Hundreds of Lisu with fear-branded faces milled around the forty-foot-high sword-ladder, which had three dozen rungs. The Lisu did not consider the festival a time for entertainment. "It is a burden. We don't want to do it, yet we must."

A great spirit had threatened them with disaster and they must obey. Blood sacrifices of live chickens were made. The men chosen to climb went through three days of mysterious preparation.

Then, as Fraser watched, three men, naked and under a spell, climbed the ladder without injury. At the top they shouted down a message from the evil spirits.

Other men heated iron chains in a fire and threw the chains around their shoulders. Again, they were protected by demon power.

The Lisu of the upper Salween were completely unreached, and Fraser knew he needed prayer power before attempting to set foot on Satan's turf. He wrote home, asking his mother to start a small prayer group to intercede for him as he and two friends made the climb. "Ten thousand feet high," he wrote in his journal. "Have seen no other humans for two days."

Snow began to fall on the magnificent scenery—a Christmas-card picture. That night they huddled, sleepless, in a booth of branches. For two weeks they continued climbing over foot-wide trails, treacherous ledges with sheer drops below. "A people waiting and in desperate need of the gospel," Fraser recorded in his journal. "So many spiritual Christians in the homeland," he mourned, "and so little prayer directed toward us." No, work among the Lisu was not going to be a rose garden. He would be a simpleton to think so, he told himself. He had to be prepared for Satan's opposition.

Shortly after that reconnaissance, he personally experienced the power of Satan. Making a temporary home in a little hamlet during the rainy season, living in a tumble-down bamboo "outhouse," he felt the slow paralysis of depression twine itself about his body and mind. Weeks passed. Not a soul in Little River was interested in spiritual things.

With the steady down-pour of the rain, his clothes sodden, depression began to seep into his very marrow. "Does God care?" he asked. "Has he forgotten me? I hoped for great results among these people, and . . . nothing."

The depression deepened until all seemed black and it was an effort to even move. *Did I mistake my calling? Five years in China . . . What do I have to show for it? Why continue to pray for the Lisu?*

Martin Luther's rhyme might have encouraged him had he known it:

> Feelings come and feelings go,
> And feelings are deceiving;
> My warrant is the Word of God,
> None else is worth believing.

Then, not once but over and over, thoughts of suicide plagued Fraser. *Why go on? I'm so alone. Why struggle to stay alive? It would be so easy to lie on my mat and not eat—just sleep. So easy to misstep on the trail . . . go crashing headlong . . . In a matter of minutes it would be over.*

The depression was so overwhelming that he knew it was satanic. "*Satan hath desired to have thee.*" Those bone-chilling words hammered in his thoughts. But he was helpless in himself. One day crouched on his mat on an earthen floor, curled in a fetal position, he saw the woven bamboo wall part. A runner had arrived from Tengyueh, with mail, which included a little magazine, *The Overcomer*. He had never heard of it, but he read it from cover to cover. The issue featured victory in Christ, overcoming "by the blood of the Lamb and the word of their testimony."

Fraser's definite resistance on the ground of the cross of Calvary brought him immediate release. Formerly, he had left everything to the Lord Jesus, which was certainly scriptural, but the present situation—and all such situations in the future—demanded action to "resist the devil" (James 4:7).

He spoke aloud to Satan, telling him to be gone in the name of Jesus. Immediately the black depression lifted, then vanished. The evil one fled. He had to! Jesus' power was stronger. Fraser's experience taught him a valuable lesson in warfare, a truth imbedded deep in his spirit—the power in the name of Jesus.

Later, when Fraser was suddenly obsessed by evil thoughts, he cried aloud for victory in Christ, and the thoughts fled instantly.

Before leaving on the eight-day trip back to Tali, a letter arrived from the States, mentioning that the prayer group Fraser had asked his mother to organize was now functioning and praying for him.

Traveling was not always easy for Fraser. Once he traveled with ulcerated legs and feet as a result of dog bites, sores from leeches, fever. One time his pony, struggling to descend a road as steep as a staircase, slipped and turned head over heels in a wild tumble. Fraser flew off, the pony righted itself, recovered, and Fraser climbed back on the shaken beast and continued to read his Chinese newspaper.

Traveling down three thousand feet into the ravine, up the other side, fording streams, swinging over flimsy suspension bridges, staying in crowded shacks, irritable and desperate from lack of privacy, he never again knew defeat as he had at Little River.

He learned that "praying without faith is like trying to cut with a dull knife." Did not the Bible say, "According to your *faith* [not your labor] be it unto you"?

He was astounded the day he discovered that the Lisu on the Burma border held the tradition of a coming king, a champion deliverer, a great teacher who would bring good news and books in their language!

The Lisu settlement of Hsiangta lay on the southern stretches of the Salween Divide, off the main road. Fraser arrived during the New Year celebration and he spent the first day alone on the mountainside, praying and reading the Bible.

The next evening as he played his accordion and sang in

the marketplace, a crowd surrounded him. When he gave an invitation, a hand shot up and a young man bravely stepped forward. Moh Ting-chang and Fraser talked for hours.

Moh was a pastry baker. Five years before, Moh's little nephew had taken a bag of cakes to sell at the fair on the great Shan plain. A white foreigner was giving away books. The boy couldn't read, but he snatched a book, hid it in his sleeve and gave it to Moh when he returned home.

For five years Moh read the strange book, drawn to the Suffering One, but having no one to answer his questions. For five years he waited. Now he could talk to Fraser.

"Who was the white foreigner?"

"You," said Moh.

Fraser had only one day to instruct Moh; then he had to leave for a Lisu village that was expecting him.

"Come back soon," Moh said. "My home is your home."

Fraser headed toward a region never visited by a Christian, where many Lisu, Shan and other tribespeople lived. On his return, he stopped at Moh's baker shop and discovered a spirit altar and incense burning before a large brass idol.

He spent time teaching Moh the catechism and was sure the baker was a born-again believer. One of the questions in the catechism was on idolatry. As Fraser taught, he waited for Moh to see the light through the working of the Holy Spirit.

Finally, Fraser felt obliged to speak plainly on the subject. Moh confessed his great fear of the gods—fear they would strike at his wife and children, his old mother.

Together they knelt and Fraser asked Moh to pray about it and ask God for courage to do what was right. Moh did, and in response to God's Word, he tore down the red and white paper strips, the idol, and everything that could be burned.

"If this is God's will I shall have good dreams tonight!" he proclaimed.

Fraser woke early, greeted his host and asked, "How did you dream?"

Moh was one big smile. "Good dreams!" he said.

With Moh's mother, however, it was a different matter. She was an opium smoker and felt disgraced socially at her son's stand for Christ. "The white man has bewitched you! You have turned against your family and ancestors. I shall jump in the river!"

But that would mean leaving her precious opium pipe, so the threat was never carried out. Moh boldly witnessed for Christ in the marketplace and accompanied Fraser when he preached. "I never knew a braver man," Fraser stated, describing the baker.

Fraser stayed in the area a month, and when he left he was able to say to the inquiring Lisu: "If you want to know more about the Lord Jesus Christ, go to Mr. Moh on market days. He will teach you."

Later he recorded in his journal: "It seems a terrible thing that so few are offering their lives for the mission field." He couldn't help feeling something was wrong. Hundreds of millions of people had never heard the gospel, yet only a *handful* of missionaries faced those millions.

He couldn't look ahead and see that one day he and his fellow workers would translate the entire New Testament into Lisu using the simplified Fraser script, so easy that an intelligent Lisu could learn to read within a month. A Christian community of several thousand Lisu would also grow in that one village alone.

The Lisu loved to sing. Fraser, stumbling along in the dark one night over a spirit-haunted trail, was actually led to Christian Lisu in the town of Water Bowl by singing. He heard them before he saw them. They sat in the dark in a little chapel and sang. None of them could afford oil for their lamps.

Everywhere he traveled, the tribespeople were not only ignorant and superstitious and fearful, but they were surrounded by an atmosphere of evil. It could be felt. "What use is there to preach or teach while the spirit power is holding them back from believing?" he asked. Prayer, much prayer, was always needed. Even prayer from a distance, from friends at home on the other side of the world was extremely important.

As he traveled from village to village, encountering those who had never heard of Jesus Christ, these words always broke his heart: "If your message is so important, you would have come sooner."

Range after mountain range, village after village, Fraser found souls without Christ. How could they be reached? Who would go?

"I need men," Fraser said, leaning over the pulpit desk and gazing down at his audience at The Firs. "Consecrated men, men willing to live a lonely life for Christ, willing to suffer and do without the comforts of civilization."

On the aisle seat, halfway down the rows, Belle's heart swelled with love and pity for the Lisu.

"I'd go," she prayed to the Lord. "I'm not a man—but I'd go! Oh, I'd go!"

"He that loveth father or mother more than me is not worthy of me." —Matthew 10:37

"When I have learnt to love God better than my earthly dearest, I shall love my earthly dearest better than I do now." —C. S. Lewis

"There are not two Christs—an easygoing one for easygoing Christians, and a suffering, toiling one for exceptional believers. There is only one Christ. Fruit-bearing involves cross-bearing." —Dr. J. Hudson Taylor

"The greatest cross is self." —Francis Fenelon

"We are too occupied with our own spiritual growth and progress. Oh, God, let us die to ourselves!" —Jesse Penn-Lewis

"We must out-love, out-serve, out-sacrifice any others who claim to have a way to solve life's problems." —Anonymous

"It was one of not a few hard lessons through which Hudson Taylor was learning to think of God as The One Great Circumstance of Life, and of all lesser, external circumstances as necessarily the kindest, wisest, best, because they were either ordered or permitted by Him." —Mrs. Howard Taylor

V.

OVER MY DEAD BODY

September 1924–October 1928

"Ungrateful child! Have you no consideration? We put you through college, paid for music lessons, sacrificed so you could have nice clothes, gave you everything you wanted! And now this!"

Belle's mother had reason to be upset, for Sam Miller had just lost his life savings in a bad business venture. He was involved in a lawsuit, facing a possible heavy fine or even a jail sentence. Her brother Murray was unemployed, and Belle was the only breadwinner in the family. "You're our only support," wept her mother.

And now Belle wanted to go to China of all things! Dear God—how awful! *What did I do to deserve this!* she thought. Only soured spinsters who couldn't find work elsewhere or fanatics and adventurers went to the mission field.

"Over my dead body! Over my dead body will you ever go to China!" Belle's mother vowed. Alice Miller took it so hard that Belle's father forbade her to mention the subject again.

Belle took time to muse upon her paradoxical mother. She had taught Belle to pray and love God's Word, yet

encouraged her to dance and act in the theater. She had
taught her to pray for missionaries and lost souls, but begged
her to be content to do Christian work at home. She often
testified to Belle that God supplied all needs, yet continued
to berate her over and over for thinking of going to China,
where she would undoubtedly starve to death.

As president of the Women's Missionary Society for
many years, Alice Miller fought against *her* daughter answering the call of God.

"Over my dead body!" And thus it happened. While
Belle was still in Bible school, her mother died suddenly
after an operation for cancer. Later Belle learned that the
night before the operation, her mother said to a friend, "I
feel that all my busy, good works have been as wood, hay
and stubble, that my daughter has chosen the best way."

But at the moment, God was directing Belle to walk
away from the sad home situation and prepare for life in
China.

Two years at a Bible school was the next step and Belle
wondered where the money would come from. Only a handful of people knew her need. Belle began to pray daily and
before long tuition for one year of Bible school plus trans-
portation was sent to her by a young woman who planned
to go to China as a missionary. Because of ill health, she had
been rejected. The money represented her life savings.

The young woman suggested Moody Bible Institute of
Chicago, though it was across the continent. Why MBI?
Neither of them understood at the time, but God knew. It
was the largest school of its kind, offering teaching and experience far beyond that of any other school.

Belle's mother couldn't rejoice with her daughter. "Accept money from a perfect stranger?" she moaned. "My
daughter—living on charity!"

On September 3, 1924, Belle stepped off the train in
Chicago and enrolled as a freshman at MBI. Only four days
before her boat had sailed from Vancouver, Belle's father
had been acquitted of the false accusation against him.

The Lord planned several surprises for Belle at the institute. She was able to room with a young schoolteacher from The Firs in a large privately situated room. First-year students were not permitted to work the first semester and Belle had counted on working. Dr. Isaac Page, a friend since her childhood, took her to his bank and Belle was given a bank book in her name with $100 in it.

"*How can a missionary afford to give away $100?*" she wondered. "*Perhaps someone left him a fortune in a will.*" Years later she discovered Dr. Page had wiped out his bank account for her.

Waiting in line for a platter of vegetables one day in the school dining room, Belle leaned against the counter, daydreaming as usual of the Lisu. Someone else was daydreaming and Belle turned casually and met the gaze of John Kuhn, a young man who washed dishes. Their eyes met, his bluer than turquoise. Something clicked. Very annoyed at herself, Belle looked away.

"No boyfriends, remember!" she scolded herself. "No mixed parties, not even a picnic. I want these two years to prepare for the mission field."

Nevertheless, everytime she carried dirty dishes to the kitchen, she looked in his direction only to discover he was watching for *her*!

During her second semester, Belle found work as a noon-time waitress in the cafeteria for employees in a large Montgomery Ward store—servant to the servants, a spectacle, actually, since all her uniforms were baggy and torn. Over a thousand employees demanded lunch immediately.

The other waitresses and the male cooks were rough and tough, and slim little Belle had to work frantically to keep up with them.

"Hey, kid, I ordered mine fifteen minutes ago! Think I got all day?"

"Miss, where is my order? This is my lunch hour, you know!"

"Hey, girlie, you with the curls, little Mary Pickford! You forgot my coffee!"

From noon to two o'clock Belle worked like a wound-up toy. In hot weather she smelled of the kitchen, and soon the noise and rush began to affect her. Filling a cup from a giant tureen of boiling hot coffee one day, she suddenly felt breathless and weak, things swam around in her vision. She felt faint. Her arm jarred the tureen, it wobbled, and she envisioned herself lying on the floor, scalded by gallons of hot coffee.

"Lord, help me!" she cried silently, trying to steady herself.

She felt a hand on her shoulder, and strength flowed through her body so that the nausea and faintness disappeared. For a moment she was in heaven, in communion with her Lord; then the commonplace closed in around her again. She was elated for days. Only once more in her entire life, during early years in China, did she have such an experience. "He is not far away—He is *here* with me in my everyday life" was the lesson she learned.

Just before closing time one day a woman executive ordered a meal. Watching Belle closely, she followed her moves and scrutinized her face. Finally, she lifted a hand loaded with expensive rings and beckoned to Belle.

"I've been watching you for weeks. You are sweet and smiling no matter how hectic it is, no matter how customers treat you. No one else is happy here. What's your secret?"

Was it possible! Here was a chance to sit down leisurely and witness since all other customers were gone.

"The Lord Jesus Christ saved me and is Lord of my life," Belle began.

"Oh, I used to believe that, but nobody can be a Christian in the business world."

Before the conversation ended the woman returned to the Lord and later enrolled in night school at MBI.

Belle loved the classes in Bible Analysis, Comparative Religions, History of Missions, Music and Practical Work. The latter assignments took her into slums, ghettos, hospitals and jails. She and "Tommy" (Ethel Thompson) set aside a half hour for prayer each day before venturing into the neighborhoods.

A Rev. X, graduate of a Bible school, who lost his faith while attending a liberal seminary, had opened a Community House in an Italian settlement. The project almost died before it even got under way, so he sent a request to MBI for "some teaching students to liven things up." He saw that "liberalism" did not seem to inspire workers like the old-fashioned gospel did. After all, what harm could the students do if he limited them to teaching the small children?

"High ideals, that's what these immigrant folk need," he told Belle and Tommy over the dinner table in his home. "You visit and bring the people in, and I'll mold them into good citizens."

Belle's eyes opened wide and she burst out impetuously, "Why, Rev. X, what a strange meeting this is! That's just like *my* story. Except that God has brought me back to Himself and I know the only way is through the blood atonement of Christ." Out of the corner of her eye, Belle saw Tommy praying. She and Rev. X held a lively discussion. As they rose to leave, he advised, "You girls are too intelligent to swallow those old beliefs."

Belle added Rev. X to her prayer list. In his Sunday school, children began to ask to receive Christ into their lives and souls were saved under Belle's ministry. He often visited the Primary Department where Belle taught, sitting in the back row, alternately scowling and becoming absorbed in her message.

Belle, physically run down from overwork, caught a virus and spent six weeks in the infirmary. Just before leaving she was called to the reception room to see a visitor. There Rev. X stood, but what a change!

"You must have been praying for me," he admitted. "The Word you preached and taught is the power of God unto salvation, for it got ahold of me and changed me. At first I added some Bible reading to my Sunday talks, but nothing happened. Then I abandoned all my 'be good, do good' philosophy and preached the blood of Christ as the *only* way for sinners, and the church was packed."

He went on to tell how he stopped the Sunday night dances. The church board of directors fired him and he took a small Bible-believing country church.

Rev. X held out his hand to Belle. "Thank you, and God bless MBI!"

The Foreign Missions Convention of the United States and Canada was scheduled to be held in Washington, D.C. the end of January and Belle yearned to go. Missionaries from all over the world would tell their thrilling stories. The President of the United States would open the convention with prayer. There would be sightseeing trips and fellowship and . . . But there wasn't a chance in a million that Belle could afford to go.

Just a few days before the opportunity to register ended, Belle was called to the office of the Director of Missions. An unknown woman had paid Belle's train fare, hotel fees and meals, even adding spending money!

"Will you go?" Dr. Grover asked.

Would she!

Belle thoroughly enjoyed the convention. The missionary stories were thrilling. Meeting like-minded people added to her missionary zeal. But afterward, she thought: Did I enjoy myself partly because John Kuhn was one of the eight students from MBI?

In December 1926, twenty-five-year-old Belle graduated from MBI and gave a valedictory message on "The Print of the Nails." She compared it to the world's attitude to Christianity: "Except I see . . . I will not believe." The print of His nails must be upon our lives, she explained. Later, on the mission field, she found exactly the same feeling among heathen people: If it cost you nothing, then it has no value.

Three months earlier, John Kuhn had sailed for China, and Belle's heart went with him, though there was no engagement, no ties except those of love. She and John were exact opposites, but both very stubborn. Belle was emotional, impulsive, imaginative—Irish! John on the other hand was full of common sense, cautious, controlled—Pennsylvania Dutch. Besides, John felt called to the far northwest of China, and Belle's heart was fixed on the Lisu tribe in the south.

"She walked in a straight line," was the description Belle's friends agreed upon. Aching from the separation, she only leaned harder upon the Lord and trusted Him to "do all things well." There was nothing wrong with being pen pals, so letters flew back and forth across continents and ocean. For two years much of John's time would be filled with language study. The CIM requested that new workers on the field not marry until after those two years.

Belle moved to the CIM candidate home in Toronto and began Chinese language study. In 1927, rioting against the presence of foreigners broke out in China, and missionaries in the interior withdrew to Shanghai, making it now impossible for new workers to enter China.

At home, Belle would stand on the front porch of their little cottage and look out over the harbor—dreaming of China and wondering if she would ever get there.

There was so much missionary work to be done in Vancouver and the Lord knew there was work to be done in Belle's life before she could stand alone in a foreign land. For almost two years she kept house for her father and brother and worked as superintendent for the Vancouver Girls Corner Club.

The Corner Club was made up of Christian business girls who banded together to win other girls for Christ. They met in rooms on Granville Street right in the heart of the city. Every noontime, business girls with their bag lunches met and purchased hot or cold beverages at the Corner Club. Belle's work was to mix and socialize, counsel, and speak in area churches to promote the club. Many girls were won to the Lord.

"What happened to you?" one of the city's lawyers asked

his secretary. "You always used to be late, up one day, down the next, worrying about everything under the sun, half the time not speaking to the other girls. Now you're happy! What happened?"

"The Corner Club," smiled the girl.

Would she mind explaining?

Her story was like many of the other business girls whose lives had been changed. Vancouver began to hear of the club.

Belle saw the influence of the club's outreach into a variety of churches in the city regardless of denomination because the club was kept nonsectarian.

The business manager, Mother Fitch, was a godly woman who also ran the club's kitchen, cooked and scrubbed and did any menial service as unto the Lord. One day during the first week, Mother Fitch stopped Belle after lunch and gave her opinion of the Women's Board who helped run Corner Club. "You preach and I'll cook!" she beamed. "Let's go all-out for souls. And I suggest you phase out the Women's Board. They don't approve of altar calls at the Tuesday night Bible classes. We don't need those women—and their money. Let's live by faith. That will also give you a free hand in the club."

A different sort of temptation, Belle thought. Why, she could be top woman here! And of course she didn't want women on the board who weren't spiritual, maybe not even born again.

"Some natures are more open to temptation than others, and mine is one," she said as she described herself during that time.

Wait—go slow, the warning voice spoke in her mind. *You are the youngest one, the newest one, the one with least experience. Wait until you at least meet the Women's Board.* But it *was* tempting.

She found the older women to be warmhearted and sincerely wishing to see girls come to Christ. They felt the business girls favored a more dignified program on Tuesday nights. Any hasty action on Belle's part might have knocked the foundation right out from under the club.

Belle prayed, said nothing, showed love, and the meeting doubled and tripled and overflowed the rooms. Belle suffered stage fright every time she faced the audience. Many times she ran to the only place where she could lock the door behind her—the bathroom—and prayed for courage to stand on the platform and speak.

Actually, she was an excellent public speaker. She had been, after all, on the stage in theater work. Before she gave her life to the Lord, Satan didn't oppose her public appearances. Now, it was different. Fears, feelings of unworthiness and panic gripped her. Again and again she turned her feelings over to the One who knew her best, and He never failed her.

"Belle Miller and her Quartet" received invitations to most of the area churches. The singing foursome was trained by Belle, using methods she had learned in music study at MBI, methods she would someday use high up a mountainside among primitive people.

Picnics, trips to the shore, hiking, seeing their superintendent as an all-around, fun-loving Christian endeared Belle to the girls all the more.

One Monday a girl named May wandered in to the club, discouraged with her job and feeling unwell physically. Belle prayed with her, then held out a small box containing printed Bible verses.

"Pick a promise," she encouraged.

Thumbing out a card May read: "My grace is sufficient for thee, for my strength is made perfect in weakness" (2 Cor. 12:9).

"*Is*—the present tense! Not 'shall be'—but *is!*" Belle cried. "Go back to your job on the basis of that promise. Claim that promise for *right now!*"

Years later May wrote: "I claimed it. Belle taught me how to lean on the Lord for the *present* need."

In April 1928, a minister from the CIM stopped in Vancouver to visit Belle and was startled to see her looking so thin and tired. "And worried and feeling sorry for myself," Belle added honestly. She worried about her father, who could not hold on to money, about her brother's unemployment, and about the girls at the club still unsaved. It was one thing to know in her mind that she should cast all her cares on the Lord, but quite a different thing to daily, hourly practice it. Such spiritual discipline took time.

"You won't be well enough to go to China," Rev. Gibb said. "I'm ordering you to resign from the club and do nothing but rest for six months."

Belle obeyed and spent the time at The Firs, sleeping most of the entire first month, even having breakfast in bed every day. All her money—twenty-six dollars—she gave Mrs. Whipple toward food. Her girls at the Corner Club had given her showers, traveling clothes and money to buy a portable organ for the mission field.

On October 11, 1928, Belle finally sailed for China, an engagement ring sparkling on her finger.

"Girls, when you get to China all the scum of your nature will rise to the top." —Ruth Paxson

"Lord, scum is the only word to describe me." —Belle, in China

"Grace that is greater . . ." —An old hymn

"God's way always leads into trial, as far as sight and sense are concerned. Humblings last our whole life." —George Muller

"Oh, my God, if the value of prayer were but known. . . ! It is a stronghold into which the enemy cannot enter. The devil is outrageous only against prayer, and those that exercise it, because he knows it is the true means of taking his prey from him. I was insatiable for prayer. I arose at four o'clock in the morning to pray." —Madame Guyon

"If I did not feel my Father's hand in the darkness, and hear His voice in the silence of the night watches, bidding me put my hand to this thing, I would shrink back dismayed." —Gen. William Booth

VI.

IF I HAD A BEAUTIFUL QUILT

November 1928—June 1930

China's millions. She saw them first as her steamer docked in Shanghai, narrowly missing hundreds of small craft in the harbor. Junks, with sails like the wings of a bat, pleated like fans, suspended from slender pole masts. High, raised poop decks teeming with fishermen hauling in shrimp and lobster. Sampans sculling along, creaky little boats with the oarsman standing on his right leg, using his left leg to alternately step back and forth on a narrow plank that activated the one oar.

China's millions. She saw them on the waterfront. Coolies hauling merchandise from ships and docks, skinny coolies with poles balanced on their shoulders from which hung loads of all kinds. Coolies staggering under the weight of sedan chairs, coolies straining the harness of rickshaws. *Ku lih*—bitter strength.

A CIM representative met her ship. On the way to headquarters Belle surveyed the teeming rivers of humanity in the street. Peddlars, with wheelbarrows piled high with bird cages, baskets of beans and chestnuts, crying out in their sing-song voices. Garbage-filled streets, with plagues of flies

57

buzzing about. Teashops bulging under ragged awnings with scholars poring over their reading materials while drinking teacups of steaming, bitter green tea. Mongrel dogs panting in the heat as misery stared out of their eyes.

Professional beggars covered with sores limped on homemade crutches, swaddled in dirty bandages. Vendors of pottery and oil and bean curd and barley sugar lined the crowded so-called streets.

Stalls were loaded with turtles and crabs, eager to escape, solemn gray clams and enormous, awkward-looking vegetables. Hole-in-the-wall theaters issued forth the most dreadful nasal wailing.

There were blocks upon blocks of railroad yards, ice houses, western-style office buildings, and in back of the business district, high walls guarded by stone dogs behind which the wealthy lived.

In the city of several million, many thousands slept in the alleys that branched off the narrow streets, like veining on a leaf. Decaying children's corpses lay in gutters where they had been thrown, a sad commentary on the value of life.

Belle went on to Kunming, the capital of Yunnan Province. John was stationed in Chengchiang, the next village. The wedding day was set for November 4.

What a reunion they had after a four-year wait! Two lives laced together in love, anchored in God's love.

"I forgot the wedding ring!" was John's greeting. "Left it home in the bureau drawer!"

"We'll buy a brass one for now," Belle laughed. "I'm not superstitious."

The very next morning John's cook and Christian companion in the work showed up with the ring. After his master had left, Yin-chang discovered the little gift box and guessing it was the ring, started down the hills and across the plain, reaching them in time.

Already Belle faced a problem of diplomacy. Two different hostesses, each disliking the other, offered a beautifully furnished bungalow for the honeymoon. How to "save face" for them both, yet keep the peace?

The question was decided by a letter from John's father with a large check to spend on their wedding. Belle and John were married in the Chinese church of Kunming, then rode off in rickshaws to honeymoon in luxury in the French hotel.

Belle couldn't wait to work among the Chinese people. In her trunks from home, besides changes of clothing, she brought a rug, curtains, enamel paint and a lovely hand-made quilt from her best friend.

As she held out her hand to Mr. Hoste, the General Director, to say goodbye before they moved to Cheng-chiang, he commented, "Belle, if I had a beautiful quilt, I would throw it in the river!"

Whatever made him say that? Did *she* say the wrong thing? And how did he know what was in her trunk? She turned away, a little upset. She certainly didn't intend to throw *her* quilt into the river.

In Chengchiang the new Mr. and Mrs. John Kuhn settled down into two little rooms over a chapel right on the busiest street. They'd traveled by train, then by *hwa-gan*— mountain chair—over trails until the sun set. The last half hour they walked in the dark, holding hands and groping with their feet, one step at a time. Across a plain in a little vale stood the city walls of mud with huge carved gates. They were closed and locked.

"Don't be afraid," John encouraged her. "The watchman knows that I would be late tonight. Come, dear, just a short walk down this cobbled street."

As he predicted, the gates were opened to them. He carried her up the steep steps to their rooms. "We're *home*, Belle, our new home! And Yin-chang has a hot wedding feast ready. Rice and vegetables and shrimp and chicken and sauce and tea and a pastry."

Belle lay on the mattress placed over a board. "I can't," she whimpered. "I'm so exhausted. . . . I feel sick . . ." The air was stifling, there were no windows, only a door which rolled back and let everyone from the street look in.

"Maybe some hot soup," she murmured, eyes still closed.

And their wedding supper was a can of good old American tomato soup!

The next morning, after a refreshing night's sleep, Belle felt renewed and was her merry self again. She didn't complain about living poor for the Lord; in fact, she gloried in it, but she saw no reason why she shouldn't make the two rooms as homey as possible.

The cook, Yin-chang, and his wife lived in two dark, airless smaller rooms at the side of the house. Clothes washed at the well in the back garden were hung on the upstairs porch. Anything that blew down to the streets below belonged to the people!

Belle decorated one of the rooms with new rattan furniture, a couch, chairs, table and her rug. She draped the beautiful quilt over her steamer trunk. "Behold—a living room! John, doesn't it look nice?"

Not long after they arrived, visitors knocked at the door. "At last!" Belle said. "We are living right with the Chinese people and now I will get to know them." She was glad she had studied the language one and a half years. Eight peasant women shopping in the market were her guests and Belle welcomed them into the pretty room. She served tea and rice cakes and as best she could, presented the gospel story. They understood! Why, they understood!

Then something happened that recalled Mr. Hoste's words with a shock. An older woman perched on the trunk nonchalantly blew her nose in her hand and wiped it off on the beautiful quilt! A greenish, obscene viscid, oyster blob on her quilt! Her stomach turned and she had to look away. Revolting!

Then a young mother held her baby carefully away from her so that a yellow stream soaked, stained, and ruined the new rug. Custom—that was all it was. They had no idea they offended her.

Belle forced a smile to her lips and bowed as they left. "Go slowly, and come again soon."

When the door closed behind them, she weakly leaned against it and stared at the mess. Anger rashed her face— anger and resentment. "And then began my struggle over *things*."

Now she understood Mr. Hoste's words. *There is nothing wrong with beautiful things*, she thought, *but if I value them more than the people—the things must go*.

She sold the furniture and rug and bought plain lacquered chairs and benches like the Chinese used.

Belle still yearned to get closer to the Chinese people, but her society-girl background rebelled against their customs and daily life. Lice, bedbugs, no plumbing, mosquitoes, lack of comforts and the little elegancies she longed for expanded the gulf between them.

"Die daily," she constantly reminded herself. "As sheep to the slaughter." And quite a few other texts were memorized as she endeavored to discipline her mind. However, nothing helped her change inwardly until she read Gal. 2:8 and began to apply it. "For he that wrought effectually in Peter . . . the same was mighty in me."

One hot summer day the Kuhns were invited to the home of a very poor Christian family in the church. Middle-class Chinese food wasn't so bad, but the very poor lived on a diet of rice and pork fat. Sitting around the table with the smell of pigs and manure rank in the air, Belle reluctantly began to eat from her rice bowl. The main dish was just arriving, a platter of greasy boiled chunks of fat. Belle's stomach heaved, she gulped once or twice and said in English, "John, must I eat it? I'll vomit for sure."

John's blue eyes twinkled graciously at the hostess and with his chopsticks he picked up the biggest chunk for Belle. "When her back is turned, give it to the dog under the table." Because of her generous offering to the dog, the flea-bag animal attached himself to Belle, sat on her feet and lounged against her legs, while millions of fleas transferred themselves to her clothes. Belle obliged him. His appetite was her escape.

Eventually, she learned to love the pork fat as a flavor for the tasteless rice.

Before her marriage, Belle had heard so much about wonderful Yin-chang as cook, valet, traveling companion and evangelist. He and John made a harmonious team. But when John's bachelor days ended, something died in Yin-chang. Now he felt he had a spoiled, critical, lazy Mrs. John to cater to.

Yin-chang tottered under a top-heavy forehead. His little hands and feet were hidden in folds of clothing. His wife was Buddha-sized, with half-shut eyes in a large slabby face. Perhaps the word "cook" was undeserved. Yin-chang boiled the rice. Beyond that, his culinary efforts included only adding sloppy lumps of soy beancurd that "tasted like fried flannel."

Seventeen miles from the city there was a collection of twenty villages on the plain in an area named Yang Tsung where no white man ever ventured. The Kuhn's, the cook and his wife and one other Christian worker started on the trip to visit the area. That night they settled into an empty attic room over a delapidated temple.

Belle was the first white woman the Yang Tsung Chinese had ever seen. She was mobbed from dawn until dusk by curious men, women and children who wanted to see, hear and touch her.

"John! There are boys hanging on to our windowsill and looking right in at us! Last night when I was in bed, I woke up to find four women feeling my ears and nose and hair! One lit a candle and said, 'Oh, she wears clothes in bed!' Another said, 'She has let down her long hair for the night!' Can't we ever have any privacy?"

"Not in China, dear," was all John replied.

During the days they preached in all the little villages and in the evenings they held open-air meetings near their temple-home. Belle played the guitar and sang with the others. One night as her husband preached, Belle looked around at the audience. There were Chinese faces as far as her eyes could see—even Chinese standing on roofs and windowsills to hear the "white devils."

These folk were hearing the gospel for the first time! *It is worth it all*, Belle thought; *it is worth all the hardships and frustrations and harassments and disappointments*.

That night they ate rice and beancurd for the umpteenth time. In the market Belle had seen potatoes, carrots, and leafy vegetables, so she said to John, "Tomorrow is our last day here. It will be a long day and we'll be hungry by nighttime. Please ask Yin-chang to add some vegetables to the rice."

John gave the order. The next morning they rose early and walked from farm to farm, singing and sharing the gospel's good news. At noon they rested, but nobody offered them food. "At least we'll have a delicious supper," Belle said, daydreaming of fresh carrots and cabbage, maybe even meat, for John had given the cook extra money.

By midafternoon, Belle's legs ached from walking, her calves rebelled and knotted painfully, and by late afternoon she hurt all over. The pain in her empty stomach was acute.

Back in their room over the temple, Belle collapsed on the bed, faint from hunger. Yin-chang set a steaming dish on the table.

"Supper, Belle," John called.

Belle jumped up eagerly and looked into the dish. Rice. And on top, dirty gray squares of beancurd. "Is this all?" she cried in disappointment.

"Could not find carrots. Could not find potatoes. Not today." The perfect cook, stuffed into his wadding like a mashed potato in its skin, bowed oh so humbly.

"I saw them for sale this morning!" Belle began to cry, threw herself on the bed and gave in to hysterics. Finally she slept, then woke at midnight.

"I could eat a little rice," she said weakly. Her empty stomach pained like a toothache.

The "perfect cook" obliged and Belle was served a steaming hot bowl of rice and perched on the top—a bean-curd! Embarrassed Belle ate it and even asked for more.

There were other things, however, that were not as easy to overlook. Yin-chang swiped the Kuhn's charcoal-burning brazier, their zinc bathtub, and Belle's treasured vial of perfume. Then to make matters worse, John sided with the cook and rebuked Belle.

Her Irish fury roused, Belle snatched up her coat and left home, running through the city street while the Chinese watched, scandalized. Surely the white people had quarreled! What terrible thing would make a wife run away! Had the white man beaten her? Where was their God that He could not help them?

Frustrated, Belle ran and ran—outside the city gates, across the plain, and through the countryside—until she could run no more. She'd show John! To think he favored a servant over his own wife!

Slowing down to a walk, she began to notice her surroundings. The country people wore older, poorer clothes and no shoes. A few fortunate older men wore thick-soled straw sandals, a loop for the big toe and a long thong tied around the ankle. Men and women wore the same style— trousers and long-sleeved tops, shiny black hair knotted into a tail.

She saw mud houses and farms, each with a threshing floor as in Bible days. The "honey carts" carried human waste for fertilizer on gardens and fields, causing a sickening smell to rise from the ground all around.

Mothers walked along, nursing babies. Children naked from the waist down played in the dusty road. She saw graves above the ground covered by miniature brick houses. Paper money by the pack, beige with squares of gold in the center, smoldered on the graves, burned to provide the deceased with spending money. Belle knew the dead were considered to be alive for three generations; then they dissolved into a spirit form.

People dressed in white trailed along behind a wooden coffin—another funeral, another soul without Christ.

As night hastened, Belle could look into the broken-down little huts and see a dozen family members around a low table eating noodles by candlelight—long, slippery dough strings boiled with a piece of bacon rind.

With a shock Belle realized what she had done. A woman alone on the road in the dark! She came to this strange country to show that the Lord Jesus Christ himself lived in her. Today she had brought disgrace upon His name. Tears filled her eyes as she prayed, "Lord, help me to go back sweetly. The servants are probably all laughing at me. I've hurt my husband. Lord, help!"

Back she went—quietly and meekly. Not much was said. Yin-chang silently reheated her rice—with beancurd on top. John offered to dismiss the cook and his wife, and it was done.

But Belle paid dearly for her hasty action. She found it was not easy to start a fire in the ancient Chinese stove. If she spilled from a pot, the fire went out. If she dropped a spoon into the fire, a cloud of fine ash flew up to the ceiling, then fell in sprinkles all over her and the food.

Daily shopping in the marketplace took hours of precious time, haggling down the prices. Clothes must be washed in water hauled up by hand from the well. And the water must be heated. Soap was unheard of.

And the ironing! Flatirons, warmed over charcoal, inevitably left black streaks on all the clothing.

"Lord," Belle prayed. "I do miss Yin-chang and his wife. Please send me another servant—but not a lazy one!"

A new girl was found and proved to be a treasure and stayed with the Kuhns for many years. Eventually she accepted Christ as her Savior. She was a cook par excellence, and best of all—she knew eight different ways to prepare beancurd!

"Satan's first choice is to cooperate with us. Persecution is only his second-best method." —G. Campbell Morgan

"When the King commands, all things are possible!" —Frederick the Great

"Archdeacon Moule was asked by a Chinese convert, 'How many Christian ministers do you have in England?' Moule estimated twenty thousand. 'Then,' said the convert, 'you could easily spare a thousand for China.'"

"Festina lente—hasten slowly." —Motto of Titus, Emperor of Rome

"Cry not out at obstacles, O Christian, for they are your power-storage rooms." —Anonymous

". . . and run not before Him." —An old hymn

"Delays are not denials." —Dr. Wayland Hoyt

"We hammer so busily that the Architect cannot discuss His plans with us." —Anonymous

"Satan rushes men. God leads them." —Anonymous

VII.

WELCOME TO ETERNAL PEACE!

June 1930—February 1934

The city of Tali, set at the base of the 15,000-foot-high Azure Peak, was the marble quarry of China. Beautiful substantial houses were built of stone. Tali had been without missionaries for a year and the CIM asked the Kuhns to move there.

"A little bit closer to Lisuland!" Belle chirped happily. "Praise the Lord!" It had been six years since she first listened to Fraser tell of the neglected tribespeople.

The Kuhns journeyed on to Tali by foot, on horseback, and in a *hwa-gan*, depending upon the topography. One-third of the way there, Belle doubled up with abdominal pain and nausea. In less than an hour she was weak and dehydrated from dysentery. They stopped at Tsu-hsiong where an American missionary took them in. There a skilled Chinese nurse, Miss Ling, took care of Belle for three weeks.

Little Miss Ling was also a midwife, trained by a well-known doctor in Shanghai. Later, Belle would bless the day she fell ill and met Miss Ling.

"I have nursed many cases of dysentery in Shanghai,"

she stated, "but this is the worst I have ever seen."

Three precious weeks wasted! Belle berated herself, curled up on a bed by the fire, clutching her stomach. A hot brick wrapped in a towel brought a little comfort. *Oh, why do things like this happen?* A handful of ashes fell apart, glowed red and gold. She stared at the fire without really seeing it.

Hundreds of thousands of souls in China were dying every day without Christ while she nursed a griping, twisting bellyache. The fire crackled and spit, the briny smoke tear-washed her eyes. She felt as useless as a hingeless door.

They finally reached Tali, a paradise compared to Chengchiang. Their new home had three large rooms, a courtyard with a garden, and trees with a beautiful green lawn all around. Lyrical birds, downy pink blossoms and buzzy sounds gave a cheery, peaceful atmosphere. Belle loved her new home. Pastor Li of the Chinese church was a kind, godly man and they loved him from the first. Two single men were also stationed in Tali whom John tutored in Chinese. Besides his tutoring, John's days were filled with his itinerating work.

Since Tali was on the main travel road, Belle often met other missionaries, world explorers and adventurers. Sometimes there was too much entertaining to do and her Bible classes for Chinese suffered. And it was vitally important to keep on studying Chinese.

Since the people of China had lived isolated from the world for thousands of years, their language and customs remained static. The language had not progressed very far from the picture writing of the Stone Age. As warring tribes and clans united into states, the various picture languages merged. Drawings were simplified. Thirty-five hundred shells and bones existing from 1600 B.C. had carved ideograms on them (idea pictures) and were identified.

By 221 B.C. the Qin dynasty standardized the writing into the Zhuan style. Belle knew that at least 50,000 ideograms existed, of which about 5,000 were common to the average literate Chinese. Chinese of different dialects used a *lingua franca* they devised as a common language.

Belle reviewed what she had learned. The Chinese language was composed of syllables, each syllable having a different tone. Mandarin Chinese had four basic tones for each syllable, which the majority of the people spoke.

There were nine dialects, though the written Mandarin Chinese remained the same. The word order of sentences was the same as English, except there were no defininte articles, no singular or plural, and no words for yes or no.

Do you like tea? I like.

Do you learn lessons? I no learn.

How embarrassing it was the day Belle meant to say to an older woman, "Here is God's Book for you to read, a precious treasure," and it came out as, "The cabbages on the floor are a memorial to your honorable grandmother."

At the end of their first year, a baby girl, Kathryn, was born. Her Chinese name, Hong En, meant "Vast Grace." Miss Ling came to attend Belle during her delivery and all went well in spite of the fact Belle had not thought it important to have regular checkups with a doctor, nor was she near one.

For two and a half years Belle and John trained new CIM workers and sent them into unevangelized areas. Then the Kuhns were asked to move and pioneer in the Valley of Yungping—Eternal Peace. Although Belle was happy about the move, John rebelled at the thought. The people of Yungping were Moslem, and their hearts hard set against the gospel. John, lover of mountain climbing and needing to be on the move, balked inwardly against being confined to a small valley.

As his disappointment increased, he gave way to depression. Souls no longer responded when he preached. Belle came down with blackwater fever and lay almost unconscious, daily growing weaker and weaker.

As John knelt by her bed, God dealt with him about his rebellion and dislike for the work in Yungping. When he

surrendered, determined to obey, Belle began to recover.
But his rebellion had almost cost Belle's life.

One day as he returned from house-hunting in the valley
of Yungping, he talked to Belle. "I've found us a home in
Old Market Village! Three sides around a courtyard, and,
Belle, listen to this: the fourth side of the house is the riverbank! A scenic spot all right! Of course the house is in
dire need of cleaning and repair, so I've hired two Chinese
carpenters to fix it up. They also agreed to make our furniture."

By now baby Kathryn was toddling around and getting
into mischief, so Belle decided to hire a Mrs. Huwang as
cook. "I don't approve of her," John objected. "You'll be
sorry, Belle."

"I need the help," Belle pleaded. "And her little thir-
teen-year-old daughter, Small Pearl, can babysit for Kathryn."

The upstairs of the new house used to be the ancestral
worship hall, with the remains of idols lying around, so Belle
cleaned and white-washed it, turning it into a bedroom. The
largest room downstairs became a guest hall to receive visitors.

Old Market was part Moslem and part Chinese. "We'll
have a hard time witnessing here," John predicted one afternoon as they stood admiring their new home and the view
of the river. "Do you suppose we'll ever have guests?"

Belle started to reply, then jumped at the sound of small
explosions, strings of firecrackers zipping, snapping, and
popping. A long parade of people marched toward their
house and through the courtyard gate. Small boys gleefully
threw firecrackers in all directions. In back of them slowly
walked the town fathers of Old Market, bearing gifts of
scrolls, trays, silk scarves, candy and food. John bowed politely and invited them inside.

"We welcome you to Old Market and wish to join the
new religion," said a spokesman, a stately man with a wrin-
kled face and a long graying goatee. "We see the new, hon-

orable pastor does not drink nor smoke and this is a fine thing. Also, we feel Buddhism may be out-of-date and we wish to learn new things."

Belle served them tea as the elderly men sat and listened to John explain. "All have sinned" was a good place to begin.

"Ah, yes, it is so." The venerable men raised their eyebrows knowingly at each other. Was not the new pastor wise and learned? Truly, tobacco led to coughing and illness and yellow teeth, and wine led to indiscretion and even violence.

"Thou shalt have no other gods before me," John quoted, and the men stirred uneasily. "Idols could go," spoke up one man. "We don't need them."

They held a brief discussion among themselves. Yes, indeed, this Jesus of the Christians was very much like Confucius and Buddha—a good man, a great teacher, a man from God. Christ's teachings will add a nice touch to our culture.

Then John dropped a bomb! "Christians may not worship ancestors. We may respect their memory, but we dare not worship them."

"What! Not worship the ancestors? That is the basis of Chinese civilization!"

The men rose hurriedly to leave, embarrassed and pained. Not worship ancestors!

After that, there were no more visitors and only a few peasants converted. On top of that, the cook spent most of her time in her room, claiming she was tired and overworked. Once again, Belle was left with the housework along with her other duties. John had been right. As always he had been a good judge of character.

Belle prayed about Mrs. Huwang for three months, and one day the quarreling lazy cook hired a driver and announced she was returning to Tali. Small Pearl cried to stay with the Kuhns, and her mother consented. Mrs. Huwang, undaunted, rode back in style to "civilization," leaving Belle very relieved.

Small Pearl was old enough to understand the way of salvation, and Belle led her to the Lord one day as they talked together in the kitchen. The girl herself then asked to be baptized. The river was plainly seen from the bustling marketplace and to avoid curiosity seekers, Belle planned a quiet ceremony in the morning.

Mrs. Kai, who lived across the road, was awake early that morning and looked out her doorway to see the Kuhn family heading toward the riverbank. In single file walked the pastor, then his wife, then a handful of Chinese Christians. Mrs. Kai stared, dumbfounded. Yes, there was Small Pearl in her Sunday dress. Oh! Oh! What a terrible thing! Pastor Kuhn was punishing the poor child! He forced her into the cold water, then pushed her head under. Then he allowed her to stand up, and all the white people were smiling their approval!

Mrs. Kai, satisfied that Small Pearl had not drowned, sped off to wake her neighbor. The two of them scurried into the marketplace and whispered the news. In no time at all, the gossip spread throughout Old Market. A delegation of irate people again visited the Kuhns, this time asking, "What did the child do that she was punished so harshly?"

John explained baptism, and the people returned to their homes still perplexed. A-eh! The ways of foreigners!

Kathryn was almost two years old when John was asked to escort a sick missionary from another station back to Kunming. Belle decided to go along with them even though headaches and backaches plagued her.

Traveling by hwa-gan over land pitted with hollows, deeps and grooves was exhausting. Soon they stopped for lunch at an inn on top of a steep hill. Typical of many inns, this one was small, noisy, and reeked with the combined smells of oily foods and crowded bodies. Belle hurried to feed Kathryn and get her back out into the sunlight. She completely forgot her raincoat on a bench. It was expensive and a great loss because it must last seven years.

By late afternoon they came upon the village of Hwang Lien Pu and stopped for the night. Belle lingered over fragrant tea. Chinese tea drinking, she read somewhere, dated back to 2737 B.C. when Emporer Shen Nong successfully relieved upset stomach, insomnia and rheumatism with herb tea. Rheumatism! She'd have rheumatism all right if she didn't have that raincoat! She looked around for it.

"John! My raincoat! I forgot it at the inn this noon. Can you send Fu-yin back for it?"

"Not now Belle, please!" John, exhausted and famished, was annoyed with the coolies who demanded "meat money"—an extra tip.

Belle's temper flared. "That coat cost me a lot of money! I don't intend to part with it. You've got to send Fu-yin!"

Sighing heavily, John's jaw tightened. "Fu-yin is needed right now to act as go-between with the coolies."

"I want my coat!" Belle wailed. "Send him back!"

"No."

"Then I'll get it myself!" Belle whirled around and stomped out of the inn and toward the steep hill.

At first the sun warmed her arms; then it was a dying brand. The west showed the dazzling colors of red jasper— deep red, so deep that the gray sky was hardly noticeable as the sun slowly sank. She began to climb, pulling herself up by grabbing roots and hummocks, hand over hand, slipping and cutting her arms.

Suddenly it was dark. *They're sitting down to supper,* she thought. *Hot tea, hot rice, maybe pork and vegetables. I'm nowhere near the top.* It looked so close. Baby Kathryn might cry for her Mommy and John wouldn't know what to do. She rested a little.

A rustle in the bushes startled her into reality and she jumped a foot. Oh, God, bandits! Men! Protect me! Alone on a mountain in China in the dark. No money, no lantern. The path branched three ways and she stopped, confused. Stinging regrets nibbled and bit her. She turned back.

How they'll laugh! How humiliating! And the memory of two years ago when she had run out of the city in the same way because of the cook flooded her mind.

A swinging light ahead bobbed closer and closer. She quickened her steps and was suddenly caught in John's arms. "Oh, Belle, I'm glad I found you! Are you hungry, dear?" he asked lovingly, as he stroked her head resting on his shoulder. "I'll send Fu-yin back early tomorrow to get your raincoat."

It was the last time Belle ever ran away.

Letter writing and diaries were part of missionary work and Belle's cheerful, humorous chatty letters won friends for CIM and accurately recorded events in her life. Her very first prayer letter to her father in 1928 set the style for all the future letters.

Belle was simply herself—innocently playing to an audience to get attention as in university days, then giving vivid descriptions, the truth about trials, a veritable salad of information plus a dash of spiritual oil and vinegar. They were neighborly letters from one to another.

By 1931, her father was mailing 500 copies of the newsletter, and later, 1700. The letters roused prayer help from the homeland as she shared Bible promises that had proven true, poems, sadness as well as gladness. "I feel like I am sitting across the kitchen table from her when I read her prayer letters," one friend remarked.

"Such imagination!" another exclaimed. "I can just see the Chinese and the country. I feel like I'm there."

Writing was an outlet for Belle the many times she was left alone. This ability would later develop into talent and into eight books that would bless the Christian world.

"Other sheep I have, which are not of this fold; them also I must bring." —John 10:16

"My sheep wandered through all the mountains and upon every high hill . . . and none did search or seek after them." —Ezekiel 34:6

God seeks men and the closer He approaches, the more men will see His holiness and his own sin. God does not terrorize. He seeks the voluntary worship of man. Demons terrorize, driving man from God, or forcing man into a bondage of fearful slavery.

"The devil always misquotes Scripture." —Anonymous

"Oftentimes,
To win us to our harm,
The instruments of darkness
Tell us truths;
Win us with honest trifles,
To betray us
In deepest consequence."
                              —from Shakespeare's *Macbeth*

Only eight persons entered the ark.
Only four persons left Sodom.

"He that hath sent me is with me. The Father hath not left me alone." —John 8:29

VIII.

THE JESUS DEMON

March to April, 1934

They left Chinese civilization and set their faces toward Lisuland. Superintendent Fraser had suggested they make a trial trip to the Oak Flat district where Allyn and Leila Cook were in charge of a small Lisu Christian church. This way, Belle would find out if her frail health could stand living on the side of a barren canyon thousands of feet above sea level. Belle had just suffered a miscarriage. Were she pregnant she could not have traveled.

Up the valley of the Mekong River in Northwest Yunnan, they rode together on horseback, stopping at what Belle called "the dirtiest inn in the world." Unfortunately, she was absolutely right. She woke at 6:00 A.M. with a churning stomach and diarrhea.

"Help me up on my horse," she insisted. "I can't stay another day in this filthy hole."

After four hours of uncomfortable riding, they reached an empty hut where Belle could rest while John kindled a fire and made hot chocolate. Back on the horse they rode up and down hills, winding like a corkscrew, until Belle's head began to spin. She closed her eyes and hung on and prayed.

Down through plunging ravines—down, down to a river valley, then up and down, they continued, in a slow motion roller-coaster trek to Old City, past massive rock ledges sandpapered by grainy winds.

Once on the trail again they suddenly heard a distant rumble. Then it came closer, closer. A boulder picked up speed, and with a thundering crash flattened trees, sending a blast of air and rock and debris flying. The huge rock bypassed them on its way to the depths of the canyon—another close call!

Peaks of 8,000, 12,000, and 14,000 feet high towered above where the Mekong and Salween rivers gashed their way down from Tibet, forming the canyons. On the banks of these fearsome, demon-filled canyons lived the Lisu.

The nearest source of help or supplies of any kind was eight days' journey away. Eight *weeks* from the nearest doctor! Belle thought of their little girl, left behind for the time being, and shivered. "Lord, are you able? Can I trust You for even that?"

The sun was setting the day they found Old Nest, a village at the bottom of a black chasm. They were made welcome in a farmhouse and served a full-course Chinese meal. Belle lingered over the good food. *How long before we eat like this again?* she wondered.

They traded their horses for donkeys. Before dawn, they began riding—up and up and up, straight as a ladder, past pine trees, then a belt of bamboo, then reaching the top. Belle gasped at the fantastic panorama of pointed peaks and deep canyons and beyond—Lisuland!

There were many ridges to cross before that. Down, down, flayed alive by flint-edged winds, each breath shallow and painful. Then up. Then down. Up, down, up, down. Once she scrambled up a bank on knees and elbows hanging on for dear life to the tail of the donkey as he climbed, kicking dirt and pebbles into her face. She picked her way carefully over a footpath, directly under massive rock formations that the rain often loosened into landslides.

They finally reached the bank of the Salween River one night and the little village of Six Treasuries. Lisuland was ruled by feudal landowners, whom Belle nicknamed "lairds" after the old Scottish system of rule.

One memorable night they stood hand in hand and looked up at the black mountain well above them. Spots of fire flickered all over the mountainside—Lisu campfires! "Ten years of waiting since I first heard of the Lisu," Belle murmured. "And now we are almost there."

They reached Pine Mountain Village where one of the missionaries, Leila Cook, lived. Though her shanty was of bamboo, she had an iron cookstove. In the summer, she grew a vegetable garden. To say Leila was surprised and overjoyed to see them is putting it mildly. Her husband, Allyn, had been gone six months, caring for a second Lisu church at Luda, a journey of eight more days up the canyon.

Two days later something happened that astonished them all, and further confirmed to Belle her call from God to the Lisu. Three Lisu from Goo-moo Village on the Burma side had fought their way up one side of a mountain range and down the other, "searching for Jesus"!

For seven days they had inched their way through snow-drifts so high they were walking on the treetops! For eleven years the villagers had worshiped a dreaded "Jesus demon" who kept them in fear until three boys decided to find out the truth about Jesus. The story begins eleven years before that search. (The names of people are fictitious).

The village of Goo-moo was in Upper Burma, a very small village of wooden huts under a large, spreading tree. The huts were built on stilts, without a nail in the entire building. The roofs were of curly silver leaves from the banana tree.

The people were Lisu, Flowery Lisu, so called because they decorated their white clothing with shells and beads.

The Black Lisu (no reference to skin) wore dark colors and black turbans. (Belle worked among the Black Lisu.) The people in Goo-moo farmed the land, raised cows and pigs, hunted bear, monkeys and other game in the jungle land around them.

Though they sometimes visited a marketplace at Towgow, two days' journey away, the people knew nothing of Christianity and had never heard of God or the Lord Jesus Christ.

One morning a young wife, Bountiful, was unable to rise because of excruciating pain that seized her insides. By the end of the day she was in such agony that even a dose of opium could not fully numb it. The next day she was too weak to open her eyes. Bountiful's husband called Mrs. A and Mrs. B, two spirit mediums. "I will sacrifice a pig," he said. "Call the demons to heal my wife."

As it grew dark, the two women began to dance on the wooden floor while a man, Tall Corn, beat a drum. The villagers crowded around the home and joined in the cries to the demons: "Come down! Come down!"

Wave after wave of evil filled the sickroom, a pulsating living power, homeless and craving human bodies, disembodied personalities who lived and moved and thought intelligent thoughts. These spirits believed in God but trembled at His name. They were so evil that they contaminated every soul they entered.

The possession happened suddenly. Tall Corn, Mrs. A and Mrs. B staggered and fell, their eyes fixed and staring. The demons had come! A harsh man's voice cried through the open mouth of Mrs. A: "Worship God! He has a Son named Jesus and two daughters!"

"He will raise the dead and give you everlasting life!" Mrs. B screamed. "Tear down the altars to demons!"

Tall Corn was normally soft-spoken and reserved. Now his voice was rough and angry. He yelled at Mrs. A: "Why couldn't you heal Bountiful? Be quick now and see to her healing!"

"You dare to scold me? Heal her yourself!" a voice from the mouth of Mrs. A hissed.

A heavy hand whacking a gong brought the three people to their senses. As usual, they had no idea what they had said. There was a babble of confusion as the villagers all talked at once, explaining the new god.

"This Jesus must be the most powerful of the demons," said the headman. "He wants to protect us and our village. Tomorrow we will hold another seance and invite him to appear."

Bountiful was better and could sip some broth. The next night the villagers gathered again, beat on gongs, danced until Tall Corn, Mrs. A and Mrs. B were possessed. "Jesus demon, come down!" they cried.

A familiar voice replied: "Worship God and Jesus. When you pray, uncover your head. Close your eyes."

"Repent of your sins," Tall Corn's demon commanded. "Don't worship demons."

At the mention of demons, the two women cursed him. Tall Corn's demon departed and for three years he could not become possessed.

From then on a steady stream of new ideas and orders came from the Jesus demon, but it was always a bit of truth mixed with error. "Keep one day in seven for rest. Stop working your farms and I will feed you. Don't drink wine. Don't bear false witness or lie. Honor your parents."

Contrary to Chinese ancestor and family worship, the latter command was absolutely foreign to the Lisu. Little by little the Ten Commandments and the Levitical law were revealed to the villagers by demons. The Jesus demon also gave gifts to help them. He told them where the bears den in the mountain. The men followed the instructions and killed a fat bear, which gave them a feast for days.

"God will provide many cows and pigs, so build them yards," the Lisu were told. The people built, but no animals materialized.

Mrs. A and Mrs. B continued to prophecy. "Jesus is

coming down to earth! All those who refuse to worship will be burned alive. Climb to the top of the mountain and wait for him. He is bringing pigs and cows and money for you."

All the villagers left their crops and camped on top of the mountain. They waited a week, fasting and praying. But nothing happened. By the time they had returned to the village, wild animals had devoured some of the crops, the birds had taken their share, and the overgrown weeds had destroyed the remainder.

One man spoke for all the Lisu: "I wish to be free from this Jesus demon."

A Christian teacher from the Karin tribe, on his way over the mountain carrying Scripture portions, stopped at Goo-moo. "They tell of Jesus," he began, but immediately Mrs. A became possessed and screamed, "Do not look at those books! They are monkey books, books for monkeys!"

And the frightened village people obeyed. The demon also prophesied the teacher would be punished. That very night he collapsed and his fever soared, nearly burning out his life. He almost died. Though he recovered, never again would he set foot in the village, although he was invited back.

Now the people of Goo-moo Village were really afraid. They realized they were under the power of a demon and began to see the trickery. "Do not plant crops this year; Jesus will feed you," the demon would tell them. They obeyed, but the entire village almost starved to death.

A young boy (later named Mark) was the only one in the village who could not get possessed, though he tried. Now he was disillusioned. The winter before, his family had food because they disobeyed the Jesus demon. The villagers who didn't plant gardens begged at his door all winter long. Mark was tired of it all. "The Jesus demon sometimes lies," he said. "I want to find out the truth about him."

One day two other boys came back from the Salween canyon where they had gone to trade in the market at Sandalwood Flat. They purchased two small Lisu books, even though they could not read them. The books told about God and Jesus!

Mark looked long at the books without comprehension and his heart pounded. Smart fellows could learn to read in two weeks, his friends claimed. "Was there no teacher who would come to Goo-moo?" he burst out.

There was none. Goo-moo had been under the power of the Jesus demon for ten years so far.

"I'm going!" Mark declared. "I'll stay until I learn to read." So Mark and a friend started out across the high mountain pass, which was rapidly blowing shut with ice and snow. Twice they were forced back, the first time almost dead from malaria, the second time from sheer terror as evil forces dogged their steps and confused their minds.

In the winter of 1934, Mark, his brother-in-law, and a neighbor vowed to try again. By now they lived in fear of the Jesus demon—his lies, tricks and plots to starve the people.

"The believers at Sandlewood Flat were happy and at peace," Mark said. "There must be a good Jesus. Somehow the devils led us astray. I'll die in the attempt, maybe, but I won't save them any longer."

The three started out in a blizzard over an unknown road to cross the Pien-Ma pass, 11,000 feet high. The higher they climbed the harder it snowed. They stumbled often, fell, ice spikes piercing their hands. In no time they were shivering with the penetrating cold. The freezing air and the high altitude pinched their lungs, making every breath an agony.

In some places the snow was so high they walked over the treetops! As they walked, they prayed to the unknown, good Jesus. "Bring us to the truth," Mark prayed over and over. Their bodies were icy cold, past all feeling, so they bit into their arms lest they freeze and perish. When they bogged down and sank through the snow's crust, they bit their way through with their teeth, breaking off small pieces of ice at a time.

Up, high over Burma, they plodded steadily on until they reached the top—more dead than alive. "Thank you, Jesus!" they cried as they viewed the snowless Chinese side of the pass. They half-rolled, half-fell—down, down the rocky sides of the mountain. Finally after several days, they came to a village.

"Yes, white missionaries are in our canyon," was the exciting news they heard. "A man and wife, named Cooke. Another man and wife named Kuhn. Go on to Pine Mountain Village."

Mark and the other two men reached the Cookes' little shanty and told their story to Leila, John and Belle.

"We brought a sack of rice," Mark explained, "and we will not go back until we learn to read the book about Jesus."

Seven days and nights of suffering over that mountain pass, Belle thought to herself, *and we have no teacher to give them.* Even small towns in America have a church on almost every corner. Eleven years this village had been under demon control, yearning to find the true God and Savior. But there was no one to send.

Four weeks passed and the three Burma Lisu studied with the native pastor. Then Teacher Simon came back from a two-year evangelistic trip higher up in the canyon. He was homesick and anxious to rejoin his fiance, who was waiting and planning the wedding.

Belle, heartsick over what she had to say, but grieving over the village of Goo-moo, put the question directly: "Simon, will you go to Goo-moo for six months?"

For a moment he struggled with himself, but God came first. He replied quietly, "I'll go." A young boy volunteered to accompany him. These two, plus Mark and his two friends, returned to Goo-moo. Joyfully the entire village gathered to hear of the real Jesus. Everyone accepted Him, learned to read and study His Word.

Four weeks passed quickly and the Kuhns were due to return to Yungping to relieve the new missionaries who were taking care of Kathryn. Leila had left to rejoin Allyn in the Luda district to the north. The interpreter she left behind was Fish Four, a tribesman whose wife was expecting a baby.

"If her labor starts before I return, why, just deliver the baby," Leila had told Belle. "You'll find a few books about obstetrics on a shelf in the corner. If the baby is stillborn, don't feel bad. All her other babies were stillborn."

Belle gasped and ran for the books. "Why, I can't deliver a baby! Oh, my goodness, look at these pictures! Just see all the complications! Dear God, don't let the baby come until Leila gets back."

But the baby was soon on its way and Belle was alone with Fish Four's wife, Grace. The woman was terrified and most uncooperative. Belle's hands shook as she tried to help Grace into bed. Grace shook her head and crouched in a dark corner of the room.

"B-b-boil some water—I think." Fish Four obeyed, but nothing happened all that day. Labor just did not progress. Belle slept in her clothes, her eyes sore and bloodshot from studying the medical books by candlelight.

'I heard of a medicine to hurry things along," Fish Four said the next morning. He was a Christian who gave evidence of God's peace in his life. He directed the chorus of Lisu singers in the church at Pine Mountain.

Oh dear, oh dear. Oh, God, do help me, Belle agonized silently. *What if I give the wrong medicine? What if I give too much? Oh, why do I have to be here when another of his babies die?*

They both prayed about it, then decided to try quinine in small doses. Within a few hours Fish Four called for Belle. She snatched up a flashlight and followed him a short distance up the mountainside, shaking so hard she could scarcely climb. *Did I kill her? Or the baby? Oh, God, help us now!*

By the time she reached Grace, the baby had arrived— a silent damp little burden lying in a pool on the dirt floor of the hut.

"Dead," said Fish Four solemnly.

As he spoke, a baby's piercing squeal filled the room! The little girl was alive and well! Fish Four's face shone with joy and he sat all night long cuddling Esther, his first live child, in his arms. Forgotten were all the years of waiting and heartache when one baby after another had been born dead. Little Esther had come to the Lisu kingdom for such a time as this: to show Belle He chooses to use "foolish things"—like her—rather than experienced Leila Cooke.

When the baby was only one month old, John and Belle knew they must return to Yungping—at least, Belle must. The Cookes were not yet back. In fact, a letter arrived, saying, "We cannot leave this place now; folks are being saved every day. We just can't leave them. Please send Fish Four to help us."

John decided to stay at Pine Mountain Village and Belle would return to Kathryn. After that—what? They didn't know.

And Fish Four? Once again Belle asked a Lisu believer a heart-breaking question: "Will you go?"

Fish Four looked down at the baby in his arms. He'd had her for a whole month. She was his only. How old would she be when he returned? He'd miss the first smile, the first tooth—everything. He hesitated only a minute or two, then, "Yes, I'll go."

Belle felt she was standing on holy ground.

"This is the hill which God desireth to dwell in." —Psalm 68:16

"Have not I commanded thee? Be strong and of a good courage; be not afraid, neither be thou dismayed; for the Lord thy God is with thee whithersoever thou goest." —Joshua 1:9

"Be of good courage, and do it." —Ezra 10:4

"For the land you gave me is a desert. Give us some springs, too!" —Achsah, wife of Othniel, Joshua 15:19

"Grace, cheap grace, without discipleship." —Dietrich Bonhoffer

"It is always a mistake to question past guidance." —Anonymous

"Few, without the hope of another life, would think it worth their while to live above the allurements of the senses." —Francis Atterbury, 17th century

"Music has great influence on those who have musical ears, and often leads to conversion." —David Livingstone

IX.

THIS IS THE HILL

December 1934–August 1937

A young Lisu man stood on the trail at dusk and smiled to himself. In the cornfield below six girls were sleeping around a fire built to frighten wild animals away from the ripening harvest. He kept himself hidden and began to sing. Like many Lisu he was blessed with a beautiful singing voice and love of music. He made up the words as he went along.

"Nighttime covers us with a blanket," he sang. "Too bad I am alone!"

He went close enough to hear the girls sit up and giggle, but he knew they would. There was no answer. They were shy and he'd had his eye on two of the prettiest for a long time. He tried again, his beautiful strong voice echoing, undulating down into the valley and back.

"Two streams flow side by side. How nice it would be to meet and flow together."

A girl's voice answered, the words welling up and down in her throat. "When there's a field to guard, a girl can't play!"

"Your friends can guard the corn. Come, sleep in my field!"

"The night is late!"

"There are many hours before the dawn."

"My father would not want me to go."

"He'll never know!"

"My husband would kill me!"

The young man's challenge grew bolder. He described the bird calls of spring, the mating of animals, his own need.

Back and forth they sang, the words turning daring and provocative. The girl left the fireside and started up the trail. She was married to a gambling Lisu who was that moment losing at a game. Drunk, he had staked his children's lives one by one—and lost. Desperate, he tried once more, this time his young wife the stake—and lost. He put himself up for grabs. In a few short hours an entire family had been sold into lifelong slavery.

Yes, the hills of the Salween Canyon needed the liberating gospel.

After John and Belle arrived back at CIM headquarters, they were thrilled to learn that Superintendent Fraser was giving them permission to move permanently to Oak Flat and release the Cookes to move to Luda, a six-day journey higher.

Satan, too, heard of the plans and did not let them go unchallenged. John fell sick with amoebic dysentery. Next, a hernia operation was performed on him in Tali by Dr. Stuart Haverson, a new missionary. Major surgery done in a native home in the interior of China!

As soon as John was able to travel, he packed for the trip, hiring eleven pack horses and mules. Goodbyes over, they headed for Lisuland and the Salween River Canyon. Dozens of times Belle and John and the coolie carrying Kathryn crawled over landslides, their feet slipping in the loose gravel. One false step, and they would not be seen again! The muleteer leading the animals that carried all their earthly possessions rebelled and wanted to turn back.

"God does not lead us into blind alleys," John said. "Unload the donkeys at each rockpile and carry the loads over."

Belle closed her eyes and repeated a phrase from an ancient writing: "If this be of God, let me not despise it. If this be of the devil, let me not embrace it."

They arrived at a shelter and waited several days to hear that the horses and their loads were safe—all but one. The mule carrying the medical supplies fell, and all the precious equipment dropped into the deepest part of the river. But they were in Lisuland.

Next day, noontime found them in a Lisu village where they actually were served bacon and eggs! Another climb down a mountain path fifteen hundred feet, then up to a shanty brought them to their future home.

"John, I've been praying for a Lisu who can speak Chinese." Belle paused to slide the pack off her back. "We don't know any of the Lisu language, and I can't imagine how we'll communicate—"

The words were scarcely out of her mouth when a man approached, waving and smiling. Job was a Lisu evangelist who spoke and read excellent Chinese.

"How did you know we were coming?"

Job beamed. "I didn't. God told me."

It was the month of December and extremely cold. They reached a landing where the mountain had been cut into and levelled out. The shanty was made of sapling trees for the four corners, with bamboo mats for walls, and logs and stones for a roof. The inside was bare.

Three-year-old Kathryn tugging at Belle said, "Mama, o-men to hsieh liang tien, chiu tseo la, gu?" (We'll just stay a few days and then leave, please?)

Cold, hungry, exhausted, they shivered in the icy wind that blew right through the walls. John turned abruptly to hide his discouragement and walked toward an inhabited hut a stone's throw away. Belle stared at the bleak, unheated shanty that was to be their home in the dead of winter, the tears slipping down her cheeks. Through the tears she saw a tattered child's crayon drawing hanging on the wall, left

there by a schoolboy. "My God shall supply all your need."
It was as if the Lord himself spoke.

She ran to the other hut and sat with John and Kathryn
beside a crackling fire and ate a bowl of hot rice. Her personal crisis was over, and she felt accepted in Lisuland as
the Christian family crowded around, petted her, loved her,
begged for Bible teaching. Two days later the pack animals
and supplies arrived and Belle was able to make the shanty
livable.

Belle's next problem: Who would take care of active little
Kathryn so Mama would be free to "mother" the infant Lisu
church? Veteran missionaries had warned her against ever
leaving a child alone with heathen who were depraved in
thought, talk and deeds. She had heard and seen enough
for herself when she lived in Eternal Peace.

God, who has a way of answering before the prayer, had
prepared a seventeen-year-old girl who would be not only
Kathryn's guardian angel but the Kuhns' cook and housekeeper and loyal companion.

Seventeen-year-old Homay knelt by her mother's bed
in the dirty little shack that was home, four miles from Deer
Pool Village. A plump little person with a snub nose and
round face, she wore her black hair parted in the middle
and pulled back, anchored under a navy blue turban.

They were the first family in that part of the canyon to
turn Christian and almost at once "the demons bit mother."
The sick woman moaned and held her head. Homay prayed
to the living God she knew. As with many of the Lisu, the
story of the resurrection had won her to Christ. And, almost
as wonderful, the teacher's words, "Yes, the gospel is for
women, too."

"Could I learn to read and write?"

"If you want to."

Her quick intelligence and curiosity had always rebelled
at her status as a woman. "You belong to your father," her
mother would say. "If he dies, elder brother may sell you.

Best to marry, make many babies, work the fields, weave the clothes and don't talk back."

Now her sick mother began to breathe hard and laboriously. Homay's brothers paced back and forth. "Well, are we going to just let her die?" one erupted angrily. "Let's call the wizard and sacrifice to the demons. Forget the Christian way."

Homay lifted her head timidly. "Jesus healed people years ago. We can ask Him to help us."

"Bah! How do we know how to pray? Maybe you're doing it all wrong. We have no teacher now, and the missionary, Mr. Payne, won't be back for two months."

The brothers railed against their father. "If she dies, it will be your fault! Everybody is talking about you!"

"Call the wizard," the poor, harassed man finally said.

"No, no, no," Homay whispered. "Oh, I can't take part in the sacrifice. I can't stay here while they do it. I won't deny the Lord." She slipped out the door and ran up the trail and sat on an overhanging rock, praying. She returned at dusk and was cruelly beaten. Her mother was dead. Life returned to normal, but the family was backslidden.

Mr. and Mrs. Payne came back to Deer Pool 8,000 feet above the Salween River. The chapel was the size of a cow shed with a thatched roof, located on a path carpeted with pine needles, on a beautiful knoll.

Homay kept track of the days and when Sunday came, she took her basket on her back and walked four miles to gather firewood at Deer Pool. This way she could slip into the chapel and sit in the back for three services and still return home with a full load of wood.

She discovered that even as a new Christian, she had a right to pray anytime, anywhere, and that prayer was a power over any bad influence of her backslidden family: for they had secretly sold her to a fellow named Philip, a nominal Christian, but shallow and spiritless.

For months Homay grew spiritually, prayer making her life vital. Outwardly, she was submissive, rising early to weave, weaving again late at night after the farm work was done.

One day she received a note from Leila Cooke: "We are moving again and the Kuhn family will live in Oak Flat. They will need a Lisu woman to cook and take care of their little girl. Would you like to go?"

At first Homay laughed at the idea. A servant? Lisu people were highly independent, free to come and go. They didn't work as servants. And her family? They would probably see her dead first.

Homay prayed about it, then saw things in a different light. If she lived with the Kuhns, she could worship God openly. Take care of a little child? That would be lovely. Like any Lisu girl, her heart longed for children of her own. Her father taunted her with the most stinging insult of all— dry tree, dry daughter. Far better to be lame or blind than a barren woman.

Homay worked even harder and faster to get the family's clothes finished. One day she said, "Father, soon I will go up to help the new Ma-ma at Pine Mountain for a few days."

He just grunted. Homay sighed with relief. She would stay and stay until her father complained. Then she would send him part of her salary!

A few Christian ladies on the other side of the globe, in San Francisco, met especially at this time to pray for the right Lisu servant for Belle. So it was no coincidence that the Kuhns, on the way to their new assignment, stopped for lunch at the very hut where Homay lived.

Belle liked Homay at once—her cleanness, her loving concern for little Kathryn, her cheerfulness. After lunch the Kuhns pushed on farther up the mountain. Belle couldn't forget Homay. At one dizzy hairpin bend of the road, they stopped to rest and Belle looked behind her. Following them was Homay, a rolled-up blanket on her back!

"I think we have found a helper," John remarked.

Was it possible? Belle remembered Leila's warning: "You will have a terrible time finding a servant. Start praying

for one." Without any fuss or problems on Belle's part, Homay was given to them and became part of the family until
her early death.

Not *everyone* had seen white people in the area the
Kuhns passed through. One little fat dumpling of a lad told
his mother he saw a demon. "All w-w-white," he babbled
through chattering teeth. "A nose *this* big! Like a bird,
Mama!"

"A-eh! Yes, some demons are part bird!"

"Terrible blue eyes! Blue!"

His mother gave a little scream and hugged him close.
"Demons steal children, darling. Don't ever go near that
spot again!"

"Mama, he smiled at me and talked Lisu!"

"That's the way demons are! Stay near home after this!"

The Kuhns knew they had sixteen months before furlough time, and they began at once to teach and ground the
Lisu church in God's Word. John built a large, sturdy log
cabin and named it Home of Grace.

In July 1935, they took a trip to villages high up the
canyon that had never been touched by the gospel. But
travel in the rainy season brought malaria upon Kathryn,
and the germ of erysipelatis lodged in Belle.

Streptococcus erysipelatis lay dormant for a little while.
In August and September while John was visiting Goo-moo
in Burma, Belle developed fever and chills. On the second
day dark-red swollen lumps raised up in her mouth and over
her body, filling with pus. They itched, burned, pained.
Belle's throat was so swollen she couldn't swallow. She suffered in the hottest months of the year, the months when
eggs and chickens were not obtainable, the "famine
months."

Belle would have given anything for a sponge bath as
she lay on the hard boards, sweating, sticky and unable to
drink fluids. Homay tried to help, but she didn't understand. She wet her hands in hot water and patted Belle's
face.

Every night the Lisu Christians prayed and sang over Belle, but she grew worse. Evangelist Job rose early one morning and set out for Paoshan for help, a six-day climb. Belle stirred wearily on her bed. *Oh no,* she thought, *only eight months in Lisuland and already my health has broken down.*

Almost three weeks passed before Job returned with a nurse and her friend. Belle was almost dead from starvation. She needed milk and eggs and meat and vegetables to revive her, so she and Kathryn were carried out of the Salween Canyon to Paoshan.

After a few months rest and nourishment, they returned to Oak Flat just in time for Christmas.

The little chapel was packed with believers for a testimony meeting that night. Snow fell gently and the warm fire inside matched the warm hearts. Three and four at a time eagerly leaped to their feet to tell what the power of the cross had wrought in their lives. Young Joseph, betrothed to Homay, let the new believers speak first, but anxiously waited his chance. In a few days he would leave to cross the Burma mountain and stay six months as a teacher to a little group of Christians there. (Homay's first fiance, Philip, had deserted her and the marriage was never consummated.)

At last he jumped to his feet. "I have nothing to bring the Lord Jesus on His birthday. But all that I am—I give back to God!"

In March 1936, the Kuhns returned to Vancouver for a much-needed furlough. John had been on the field ten years without a break; Belle, eight years.

The saddest letter they received while home was about Homay and the beloved Joseph.

Joseph had lived as a heathen in the village of Dried Fungus. When native Lisu evangelists brought them the Word of God, the entire Tea family was converted. After the teachers left, sickness and misfortune struck the Tea family. "The demons are offended! Sacrifice!" they told each other. And they renounced Christ—all but twenty-year-old Joseph.

"Get out!" his father yelled. "The demons will be angry if you live here and worship God."

Driven into the lonely mountainside, Joseph found a deserted hut and lived alone for months, trapping small animals and drinking water from a creek. Soon he was sick. A passing Lisu saw him and told the old father, who climbed up the cliff to see his son.

"Son, come on home. I'll sacrifice a pig to the demons and they will send healing."

Joseph, ragged, miserable, half-starved, shook his head. "I am not afraid to die, for God is my Father. I am sure of a place at God's right hand. I will never sacrifice to demons."

Joseph recovered and a short time afterward led his entire family back to the Lord. Five years later he met Belle and John and fell in love with Homay. The wedding day was announced. By then Joseph was an eloquent preacher, who kept his audience on the edge of their benches as he dramatized the Old Testament stories.

For a year's work as evangelist he received room and board and fifteen dollars. Poor as he was, he proposed to the prettiest, most sought-after girl in the canyon, a girl who had almost fifty offers of marriage—Homay. And she saw beyond the poverty to the shining soul of the man and accepted.

A few days after the Christmas service of 1935, Joseph set out for Burma while Homay waited at Oak Flat. In six months of teaching on the other side of the mountain, souls were saved, a church established and Lisu leaders trained and able to continue on their own.

Joseph and his two companions, Samuel and Lysias, started toward home—and Homay. It was July, warm, and they went for a swim. Joseph floundered out beyond his depth and drowned.

It was Leila Cooke's sad task to break the news to Homay that Joseph would never stand beside his beloved at the wedding altar. Never again on earth would she see his dear face.

Homay ran to a deserted little hut to be alone, and the missionaries could only pray and wait. But everything was all right. They heard Homay singing:

"Have thine own way, Lord,
　Have thine own way."

Before Belle and John could return to Lisuland, war broke out between Japan and China and all sailing was canceled—except that of the Kuhns. The heavy fighting was in the north and the Salween Canyon was in the southwest. The CIM superintendent approved the return of the Kuhns and one other couple. They sailed August 31, 1937.

"They that are Christ's have crucified the flesh with the affections."
—Galatians 5:24

Belle learned to hold her loved ones, not clutched tightly in her fist, but on the palm of her hand, so that when God claimed them, it would not hurt so much.

"After crosses and losses, men grow humbler and wiser."
—Ben Franklin

"The word of His grace which is able to build you up."
—Acts 20:32

"The kingdoms of this world
Have become
The kingdom of our Lord,
And of His Christ,
And He shall reign
Forever and ever.
Hallelujah!
Hallelujah!
Hal-l̯-l-a-a-a-looooooo-jah!"
   —Revelation 11:15, sung Lisu style

"Notice among yourselves, dear brothers, that few of you who follow Christ have big names or power or wealth."
—1 Corinthians 1:26, The Living Bible

"The Christian is like the ripening corn; the riper he grows the more lowly he bends his head." —Thomas Guthrie

X

THE RAINY SEASON BIBLE SCHOOL

September 1937—1942

A telegram was waiting for Belle in Hong Kong, which plunged her into despair. Time stood still, was no more, and the moment of grief was frozen in stone to last forever. Belle had looked forward to placing six-year-old Kathryn in a school in Kunming, not too far from Lisuland. The telegram from the CIM headquarters read: "Send Kathryn to school in Chefoo." Chefoo was a seaport in northeast China. Kunming was in southwest China. True, the Chefoo school was bigger and better, in healthier climate, but in essence it meant giving Kathryn up perhaps for life.

Belle went through the next few days in a state of shock. "The last time . . . the last time . . ." she agonized. "The last time I will ever give her a bath . . . the last time I listen to her prayers . . . the last time we play together in the sun . . . the last day . . . the last few hours . . . the last kiss . . . the last hug."

Kathryn's ship sailed and Belle was torn. She grieved so much that John walked the streets with her until she exhausted herself enough to sleep. Everywhere she looked, she saw her little Kathryn—saw her holding her rice bowl

101

under her chin and expertly flipping her chopsticks, heard her singing, saw her sitting on the doorstep with a little friend, saw her in the marketplace picking out the biggest lichee nuts, saw her . . . saw her . . . yet didn't see her—until she thought she'd go mad.

Belle and John sailed from Hong Kong to Haiphong, through French Indo-China by train into Yunnan, to beautiful Kunming, 6,000 feet up. During the long trip the Lord comforted Belle, reminding her she was a soldier, that faith was sometimes a fight, that what happened was for Kathryn's best interests, that Belle should not cling so tightly to her loved ones. Finally Belle left Kathryn in the Lord's hands.

A lesser disappointment was waiting for Belle when they met with Mr. Fraser, but still it was a great disappointment. They would not be returning to Lisuland, but would take up residence in Paoshan. "I need John as my assistant for West Yunnan," said Mr. Fraser. The Christian church in Lisu was tiny and a Miss Emberry was doing a fine job. Belle was heartbroken all over again. Not return to the Lisu?

She opened her Bible, asking God for guidance. As she browsed through Zephaniah, chapter 3, a few words caught her eye and she was convinced it was for her. "I will bring you again." That's all, but she had prayed about the Lisu church and God said, "I will bring you again." After praying, she knew it was His promise that they would one day return.

On October 27, they arrived in Paoshan and settled down to work again among the Chinese. Only four weeks later came the letter that set Belle dancing for joy, literally dancing around in the bedroom with the door carefully shut so John would not see!

"Please return to Oak Flat for a few months. The church is ready to split apart and needs some sound Bible teaching." There was a cautious postscript: "This is not a permanent assignment, remember."

On December 3, they packed and climbed the west side of the mountain outside Paoshan. They didn't know it, but the "temporary assignment" would last for years. In September 1938, Mr. Fraser died suddenly of malignant cerebral malaria and all missionaries stayed wherever they were located.

On May 28, 1938, the first RSBS (Rainy Season Bible School) was held in Oak Flat during the three months of the year when farm work consisted only of camping out in the fields to protect the crops. The Kuhns returned from furlough to find the Lisu church bordering on legalism as they did not have the entire new Testament in their language, and did not understand Law and Grace. (The complete Lisu New Testament was not published until 1951.) Belle did have the four Gospels, Acts and the Lisu New Testament in manuscript form.

She brought back a portable typewriter that typed Lisu script, and Homay was promoted from cook to secretary. She made a copy of the Bible portions to be studied for each student. So many words were new conceptions for the Lisu. "Conscience," for example. They did not know they had a conscience until they learned the word from the Bible.

Belle and John and a new missionary, Charles Peterson, knelt in prayer for the RSBS and Belle spoke for the three of them when she prayed, and no one questioned her logic: "Oh, God, this is a new venture for us and we feel like three zeros. But You are our leader who goes before us. You are Number One in front of the zeros. And that makes one thousand!"

Monday morning came and the students began arriving from all directions. Up and down the rocky mountain canyon they climbed, over a path through pine tree groves, on to the brow of a cliff with a long drop below. A collection of little shanties plus the missionary house made up Oak Flat Village. Barefoot boys and men lugging sacks of rice and sleeping bags slid down slippery muddy paths, some boys eager, some reluctant, some happy and some glum, but all perspiring and glad to see Ma-ma and Ma-pa.

Thirty-eight-year-old Job, a Christian eighteen years,

was the oldest and the first one to meet the Kuhns the night they arrived in Lisuland. Next came Luda-Peter, age twenty-five, handsome and poised. He was a good song leader winning three families to the Lord when he preached in the village of Water Buffalo.

John and Belle then began to greet the others as they came in. Silas, who was twenty-three, just couldn't remember the lessons, but he would describe in meticulous detail some insignificant point of doctrine. Lucius, also twenty-three, seemed bright and quick. Nathanael, twenty-two, was right at the bottom of the class in reading and writing, but able to give thoughtful sermons from experience.

Then came Cho-a-tsch, the clown, and Rufus, the cowboy. Next to arrive was impetuous Jonah who spoke first and reflected later. Titus, who drew pictures all over his books, and Aristarchus, who left a job paying $60 a year to enter Lisu ministry for $16 a year, cheerfully greeted the Kuhns whom they grew to love and respect.

In all, twenty-some Lisu, mostly men, attended. (Women did not attend *en masse* until 1943 when, despite stormy weather and a war, 33 Lisu women enrolled. Belle was alone then; John was in Japanese-held territory, trying to rescue a missionary couple.)

In 1938, Belle also found time to write her first book, *Precious Things of the Lasting Hills*.

As the RSBS grew in grace they multiplied the gospel by fanning out on preaching assignments into twenty villages around them. The first weekend the students reached 500 new Lisu, the second weekend 700, and each weekend the total climbed.

Music was certainly not lacking among the naturally musical Lisu. On one occasion a bright Lisu lad even went so far as to practice the Hallelujah Chorus from Handel's "Messiah" on the astonished pigs behind his cabin.

The Spirit helped the infirmities of the infant church (Rom. 3:26), and Belle saw the evidence as she listened to the prayers of her students:

"Lord, Thy name is written on my heart and my name is written on Thy hands, so we cannot be separated."

"Lord, Thou hast given to me eternal life and I am Thy slave. But You have called me friend."

"Forgive me, Lord, that I only asked things from Thee. Now I want only what You want me to have."

Closing Day ceremonies were held with the students voting for valedictory speakers, complete with certificates, corsages and organ music. One graduate *cum laude* dyed his white sneakers with beet juice and gave a talk on Satan's appearances throughout history. Job caused the audience some merriment when he held up a white cloth to explain how the curtains of the Tabernacle were made of goat's hair. (Goats in Lisuland are black!)

Junia, who wore all the clothes he owned to be sure he got the right combination, gave a five-minute talk on a book of the Bible he had studied. He concentrated heavily on not perspiring.

Sometimes during RSBS if it was sunny, a school picnic was held on Sunset Ridge facing west where they could light a bonfire and roast corn and watch the sun set.

The gathering ended with the singing of "Hallelujah, What a Savior" in harmony. Belle planned a consecration service around a campfire one night, and even though it was in the rainy season she prayed, "Lord, could You stop the rain and give us a sky packed with stars for this serious occasion?" He not only stopped the rain, He added the most gorgeous sunset they had ever witnessed.

John spoke on "sacrifice" and every student knelt in consecration, promising to live wholly for God from that night on.

Dear Gad, with his deep bass voice and almost total inability to learn, begged to accompany an evangelist. "He is so recently saved out of a life of sin," Belle said to John. "Shall we trust him?"

They trusted, and Gad set off for his hometown of Squirrel's Grave, determined to be a witness, if not an accomplished preacher. Clumsy in speaking, slow, panicking when his mind went blank (which it often did), Gad never stopped witnessing, even when he developed mumps and his throat all but closed.

Eventually a new RSBS building was built, which Belle christened "Hephzibah," roughly and symbolically translated—"the object of God's affection."

The RSBS was entirely Belle's idea and probably her most important contribution to the work in Lisuland. One of the most important results of RSBS was that the Lisu Christians became mission-minded!

An unreached tribal land called Yongpeh lay to the east in a gorge of the Yangtse River, a two-week journey away. A missionary living near Yongpeh wrote and asked the Kuhns for help. "There are Lisu here who need to hear the gospel in their own language." The request arrived just as the first RSBS ended.

Belle brought the letter to the attention of the Lisu church in Oak Flat. By now the elders were used to making decisions after prayer, and little by little took on almost all the responsibility of church government. Even to the extreme, sometimes, of appointing one of their own to preach at the Sunday morning service, leaving Ma-ma and Ma-pa sitting in the audience.

The Lisu church sent out Aristarchus and Secondus to answer the call at Yongpeh. They walked all night long to avoid being "drafted" by soldiers searching the hills for recruits. Tired, cold and close to breaking down, they reached Yongpeh City, somewhat like Paoshan, with many lepers and a big market where thousands of Chinese as well as the Lisu came to trade. Only a half day's trip away lived the Lisu, too many to be numbered.

The young evangelists borrowed a house and held services. They visited the outlying Lisu, village by village.

"Pray for us," the tribespeople said. "We never heard this story before."

Aristarchus and Secondus found the Lisu dialect different, but as they prayed and kept on in faith, God gave the understanding. They also made an important discovery—the forbidden territory, the tribe of Lolo, who were feared by the Chinese. The CIM had been praying for the Lolos since 1928 and earlier. These bandits and war-like aborigines, consisting of more than 100,000 often kidnapped both Chinese and Lisu.

The two youths sent an urgent letter to Belle: "Please, Ma-ma, may we stay longer? We have so many calls to preach we have separated and travel alone. All we have time to do is tell the way of salvation, teach a prayer and a short song, then go on to the other calls. We are afraid that when our backs are turned, Satan will pounce upon these new believers, and how will they continue without His Word?"

Soon word came again from Aristarchus and Secondus that 35 families (about 200 persons) were converted and had turned from idols to the living God.

And wonder of all miracles—the Lolo tribe actually invited the Lisu evangelists to preach in their village!

Belle recalled Mr. Fraser's last request: "Try to get the gospel into the Yongpeh district."

A top official named Chiu Teh-tsi was the first in the Yongpeh area to receive Christ. He wrote to Belle, telling her he had been seeking "the truth" all his life. Now, he had peace. He reported forty families who cast down their idols, but thousands still did not yet believe.

Aristarchus also wrote the Kuhns, reporting about 250 Lolo Christians were already hard at work building a *third* chapel for the teaching of God's Word.

Belle had not the heart to call the boys home, yet they needed more Bible study themselves. How poverty stricken and helpless she often felt when calls for the gospel came from all directions and she had only new converts to send.

"We'll send our best," John decided. "Our top student, handsome clever Luda-Peter."

"I thought of Gad," Belle suggested.

"Gad!" John snorted at Belle's lack of judgment. Gad

was a scowling, impossible-to-teach beginner, but Belle watched his daily life, which spoke louder than his appearance. Luda-Peter's mind was on his upcoming marriage and he demurred. But Gad's face lit up with joy when he, along with Daniel, was asked to go for a year of hard labor. Gad's one leg was a mass of ulcers from ankle to knee. Twelve days of mountain climbing lay before them.

"It will soon heal," Gad pleaded.

Up and down cliffs, over narrow trails, in a land of different customs, dialects and food, without encouragement or reward, Daniel and Gad plodded on, braving demons in heathen villages. As with other evangelists who started out two by two, calls were so numerous they often separated. Six hundred Lisu in Yongpeh were now Christians. Daniel and Gad won over a hundred persons to Christ in that year.

The year of preaching matured Gad, though he never did learn to speak without mumbling, his main message being, "We must not sin!" Belle sent him alone to Hollow Tree, a four days' journey to the south, the most difficult spot of all. A few months later Gad was dead from an unknown fever.

He knew he was dying and as people crowded around him in that strange land far from home, he said in his flat, unemotional way, "All of you behave yourselves." He died, giving the Bread of Life to the starving.

Year after year the Bible school grew in spite of illness among the staff and lack of teachers. During the years of World War II the Japanese were just over the mountain ridge, breathing out threats toward all missionaries.

Beginning in 1937, the Japanese took province after province from General Chiang Kai-shek. While Chinese waged a civil war against Communism, Japan helped herself, finally taking Burma in 1941.

The most awful experience of Belle's life loomed nearer.

In 1942 the Japanese captured the CIM school for missionary children at Chefoo and little Kathryn was taken from school and interned in a prison camp, along with Mrs.

Fraser and her three daughters.

Stories of Japanese atrocities made headlines in the civilized world: RAPE—TORTURE—MASSACRES—STARVATION! Belle and John could only claim God's promises and discipline themselves not to dwell upon their fears.

Mercifully, God hid from them the knowledge that six years would drag by before they would ever see Kathryn again.

"The need is the call." —Anonymous

"And behold, I am with thee, and will keep thee in all places whither thou goest, and will bring thee again into this land; for I will not leave thee, until I have done that which I have spoken to thee of." —Genesis 28:15

Moses had to have human help *in intercession.*
—Exodus 17:11–14

"How should we know
What it is all about?
Go to the men that sowed the crop,
We only threshed it out." —Anonymous comment on feuds

The carnal church: "Envying, and strife, and divisions."
—1 Corinthians 3:3

Caste, clans, class—all weights which must be laid aside.

"Tell of success, people give to success," is the rule of thumb when writing missionary letters. But Belle's letters and books also told of the failures.

"I have heard people say they enjoyed hearing about missions. I often wonder if they would enjoy watching a shipwreck." —Mrs. Robert Stewart, China

XI

BURN THE CLAN ARROWS!

1939—1940; 1942

A three-week trip in November 1939 turned into a three-month stay when Belle and John were asked to visit the Three Clan Village in Luda district to settle a feud. Riding mules, taking native evangelists Luke and Lucius, plus two deacons, praying for revival, the Kuhns traveled on for six days. The last part of the trip was along the river road. It was a beautiful day, with a blazing sun overhead and wispy clouds trailing like smoke. The warmth of the sun felt good on this cool day.

The rock formations fascinated Belle—some as bleak and puzzling as Stonehenge, some colored and chipped and sliced. She saw gold-amber flecked stones, like citrine, needled through with color; others, a hard gem green. One ledge was the brown-black swirling color of petrified wood, below were caves and crevices, whose end she could not see.

Around the corner came a parade of people leading a horse trimmed with red ribbons and bells. "For Ma-ma to ride." The leader of Clan One bowed low, hoping to make the first and best impression.

Clan Two, hoping to rival the other display, was farther
along the path with another delegation—the spokesman sa-
luted John and handed him a written invitation for supper!
Another jolly fellow offered Belle a drink out of a teakettle—
cold honey water with scraps of wax floating in it.

Clan Three made the very best impression on this rather
cool day with *hot* honey water. Where a river crossing must
be made, the people had built two rafts so the guests would
not have to use the rope bridge.

On the opposite bank more than a hundred villagers
waved a welcome. "All this loving concern and affection,"
Belle murmured to John. "I'm afraid it's all part of the feud."
Still, it was the grandest reception they ever received.

Just what was the feud all about? A few acres of valuable
wormwood trees. John and Luke met with the three clan
elders and tried to divide the land fairly. "Please do not go
to the heathen official," John pleaded. "Accept the church's
decision. Suffer loss rather than quarrel before the unsaved."

The stony-faced clan elders balked and shook their
heads. Not one clan would give an inch. They appealed to
the Chinese official over their area. His Highness arrived in
state, carried on the shoulders of Lisu clansmen (forced
labor!), demanded a feast of roast pig, returned home (after
doing and saying nothing), and sent his bill: First, a $200
tax for "weariness of the feet" (while he was riding piggyback), then a tax for passing judgment, then a tax for writing
out a document, then another visit would be required, another pork feast, and a few taxes, which he obviously
thought up on the spur of the moment. The total sum ex-
ceeded the value of the land. The clan elders sat in gloom,
holding their aching heads.

Not even the approach of Christmas cheered them up.
For Belle it was the happiest Christmas of her life as she
held in her hand her first Lisu New Testament, a new pho-
tograph of Kathryn, and a box of candy from America.

Luke and Lucius and the two deacons left for their

homes in the southern part of the canyon leaving Belle and John to cope with the ongoing feud.

For a while the fight was forgotten in the excitement of an announcement John made in church: "We are going to hold a February Bible school for the entire month and runners will go out all over this area to invite everybody! I want you people of Three Clan Village to each take one student into your homes and feed him for the month. Will you do it?" (How better to break the narrow law of the Clan than to entertain strangers?)

Hands went up all over the chapel. The Christians of the village were kind-hearted, but they were under the bondage of the clan. If a clan member wished to peddle opium, steal pigs, commit murder, kidnap a wife, all members of his clan were pledged to help him.

Belle and John began the February Bible school and even though a plague of typhus threatened, not one student left. Belle, however, sensed something was lacking. No sooner had school closed than the old feud burst into flame. People again took sides, quarreled and put themselves under the law of the clan.

What had all our teaching accomplished? Belle wondered. *We live our lives before them and present the Word, and what have we to show for our three-month work here in Three Clan Village?*

John reasoned with them concerning the feud, and they actually shook under conviction. But where was the *power* to set them free?

Two days remained before the Kuhns would leave the feuding village that professed to be Christian, having changed nothing or no one.

In a small town back in America lived three elderly Christian women, separated from each other except by phone. Mrs. A had received Belle's prayer letter about the feuding clans and she just couldn't stop thinking about it. She phoned Mrs. B, who was blind, and said, "I can't stop thinking about the three clans. Will you take time to pray for them right now?" Mrs. B agreed, and phoned Mrs. C, who was ill. She, too, agreed.

The three women, each in her own home, began to pray. For them it was morning, for the Lisu it was evening. Sometime in that twenty-four-hour period, John held one last meeting before leaving Three Clan Village. He spoke on "The Law of the Clan and the Law of Love." Belle cut out two sets of paper arrows. On one set she wrote, "I have no desire to practice the law of the clan"; on the other, "I desire to practice the law of love."

As John spoke, he pointed out that the law of the clan was a chain Satan used to tie their hands and feet. In the audience were the top twenty elders of the clans. There were two brothers who hadn't said a decent word to each other in twenty-six years. John ended his talk and advised: "If you want to break free from the law of the clan—centuries old—come up and throw a paper clan arrow in the fire. Then take up a love arrow to show your promise to follow the law of Christ, which is love toward *all* men, not just those of your own clan."

There was hostile silence. (The ladies in America were praying diligently at that very moment!) A clan leader rose to his feet and walked the narrow aisle between the taut figures, picked up a clan arrow and dropped it into the fire. As he took his love arrow, he faced the other men and gave a ringing testimony. One by one, all clan elders—except one—renounced the custom of men that imprisoned their spirits, and were set free by Christ's perfect love. All except one, the most powerful, stubborn man in the village, the one who most coveted the forest of wormwood. His name was "Lamb." If ever a man was misnamed, it was this clan leader.

Disappointed, John began to close the meeting. "I guess Lamb is not one of us, since—"All at once Lamb stood up and apologized sincerely to an elder he had hated for years. Belle held her breath. Would he follow the others? Walking forward with a determined step, he burned a clan arrow and received a love arrow. Belle gave a sigh of relief and lifted her head in thanksgiving to God.

On the other side of the world, the three ladies stopped praying and sensed something remarkable had happened. One of them wrote down the exact time and date and sent it to Belle.

Belle also wrote down the time and date. "Dear," she said to her husband, "your quiet speaking to them could not have accomplished this miracle alone. Somebody, somewhere, was praying for us just then."

Two months later, Belle opened the letter from Mrs. A. The times and dates matched!

Belle turned to her Bible and discovered that according to Matt. 17:21, some demons were stronger than others; thus, a situation might require stronger prayer and more people praying. Once again she was reminded that missionary work needs prayer warriors behind it.

In February 1942, the first Bible school for women began. One of the students was Sah-me-nyio, the Blind Singing Girl of Deer Pool Village. Sah-me-nyio, her parents and two sisters had all accepted Christ the first time they heard the gospel. Sah-me-nyio was not blind then, and as she herded the cows up and down the hills or spun cotton she sang the choruses and hymns. She had a reputation for being the happiest girl in the village.

She thought nothing of it at first, when her eyes began to itch, just rubbed them hard with her sooty hands. Her father had trachoma, but Sah-me-nyio knew nothing of the infection. Her eyelashes began to grow inward and things around her became less clear until finally she could hardly see anything at all. Still she sang and gave testimony to her faith to anyone who would listen.

"How can she sing and still be happy?" visitors asked, staring at Sah-me-nyio, who sat outdoors often sharing a hymn. And so she came to be known as the Blind Singing Girl of Deer Pool Village.

Twenty-four female students arrived on the first day of the Bible school, among them Sah-me-nyio. Belle had four rules: The girl must be a Christian, at least seventeen, able to read and write, and recommended by a deacon of her village.

At one time Sah-me-nyio could read and write, but now she was almost completely blind. Belle welcomed her anyhow, and Sah-me-nyio moved into the "dormitory" with two other girls from Deer Pool. Dormitories in Belle's school were shacks with a wooden plank for a bed and three rocks for a fireplace.

Sah-me-nyio received a new Bible name, Leah, because it was easier for Belle to remember. Also, the new name was significant, Belle explained, telling her about the long-ago Leah with eye trouble, whose ally and refuge was God.

"Please, Ma-ma," Leah said, "when you send me across the mountain on teaching assignments, may Tabitha and Abigail go with me?"

Belle swallowed the lump in her throat. She hadn't dreamed of sending a blind girl traveling over treacherous trails, but since Leah was willing, she gave her consent.

None of the girls had ever studied to take an exam, nor had any of them ever attended even the simplest school or class. Part of the exam was to recite chapters of the Bible from memory. Leah could neither see to read nor take notes, yet the only girl who passed all exams with first-class honors was blind Leah!

She and her two friends returned to Deer Pool Village, promising Ma-ma they would use the powerful weapon of prayer. Satan struck hard at the blind girl. Her only brother died of tuberculosis, and shortly after that Leah lay dying with typhus. She called for her family and said, "Two things I know—that God loves us, that God is faithful. When I am gone, keep God's honor high. Don't complain, go on believing. I shall wake in the Land of Light."

That March when John was away at a conference in Chungking, Belle developed a raging toothache. It throbbed in her head until she wanted to scream. Painkillers didn't even numb it. The nearest dentist was at Kunming, a two-week drive across the Burma Road. With Lucius as escort, she headed down the canyon toward Paoshan, covering thirty miles a day. Spring weather coaxed the peach trees to blossom into pink froth, and all along the path rhododendron spread their shiny leaves.

Three days later they were in Paoshan and Belle continued on with two American airmen, members of the Flying Tigers, in their private car! Belle sighed happily and dashed off a quick prayer to her heavenly Father for His kindness. No riding on the Burma Road on top of a Chinese truck, sitting high on the luggage and crossing fingers for luck as the truck coasted down grades (to save precious gas) and flew around curves.

The Americans were polite but battle-weary. "Rangoon fell to the Japs," they told her.

Up at 4:00 A.M. and groggy, Belle took a quick peek into her Bible. Genesis 28—just the Jacob Ladder story. "I will bring thee back into this land." Startled, Belle read it again. Of course He would bring her back; she was only having a tooth pulled! But unknown to her, enemy soldiers would intrude even into the Salween Canyon hunting for foreigners, and it would be *six months* before she would see the Lisu again.

On the fourth day the car broke down and after a two-hour wait, a white man driving a jeep picked them up. Arriving in Kunming, at the home of her sister-in-law, Belle found only the Chinese maid, Eva. Belle enjoyed a marvelous supper and then curled up in a real bed. As she lay there, she made a remarkable discovery: now that she had time to think of it—her tooth had not ached since she left Oak Flat!

The Lord wanted me out of there for some reason, she thought. The next day she had a dizzy spell and felt sick

with pains in her face and head. The abscessed tooth itself
did not hurt since the nerve was dead, but all the others
ached as the poison spread throughout her entire body. Gan-
grene had set in.

"If you had waited twenty-four more hours, you'd be
dead," the dentist stated soberly.

By then John was in Lashio and the doctor wired him to
come immediately. No sooner did John leave Lashio than it
fell to the Japanese. After a very short time with Belle, John
returned west to warn other missionaries to evacuate. "I'll
be back in a few days," he promised. A week later the Japanese bombed Paoshan without warning in the middle of
the day while all the families were shopping in the market;
15,000 were instantly killed. Thousands of refugees jammed
onto the Burma Road, fleeing the bombers, and John was
trapped among them.

Some time later he returned to Belle but soon left
again—this time for Tali to rescue missionaries. While he
was gone, one day Eva ran to Belle's room, crying, "The
Japanese are coming at us from three directions and Yunnan
Province will fall!"

The British Consul sent word to Belle. "Go north with
the RAF convoy!" he ordered. Three times in one day he
sent the message. "Get out while you can—that's an order!"

But Belle had received no order from the Lord. After
thinking about the doubts and fears, she gave in to the advice
of others. So on May 17, she and two other women and a
child lined up at the airfield where the convoy trucks
parked. Twenty-one-year-old Eva, who looked fourteen,
sobbed her heart out. "If only I could go with you!"

But that seemed impossible! There was hardly enough
room for white women let alone a Chinese.

An RAF officer waving them through asked, "What's
wrong with the kid?"

"She doesn't want to be left behind."

"Oh, go ahead. We can squeeze her in."

In the truck, Belle sat on top of the ammunition and

nibbled RAF rations. Seven days and nights they bumped along, and all the time Belle prayed, "Lord, You promised to bring me back to Lisuland!"

"China will fall," predicted the RAF men. In Luhsien, Szechwan Province, Belle heard one piece of good news. The children in the CIM school in Chefoo were treated very kindly by the Japanese.

Weeks went by and Belle realized their flight had been all for nothing. Yunnan did not fall to the Japanese—it was only a rumor!

One morning Belle walked out to a Chinese graveyard where she could pray undisturbed. "Four problems, Lord, and all of them seem impossible. I need money to get back to John. I need word from him advising me to return. I need a truck going in that direction, and please, Lord, I would like a female companion. You know how those men act."

Within twenty-four hours all four "impossibilities" were solved. Money came in the mail, a telegram from John, Eva begged to go with her, a convoy of three trucks agreed to take them.

Lest anyone think it coincidence, Belle made a note in her diary regarding the money. The money came as two checks, each for $50, mailed six months apart, yet arriving in the same mail!

Belle prayed on Sunday, and the Lord answered so quickly that she was able to leave Luhsien on Wednesday. The driver stopped all along the road and picked up "yellow fish" (illegal hitchhikers). More than once he threatened Eva with rape. Belle clung to the girl and prayed furiously. Finally he stopped on a deserted road to pick up some prostitutes. "There isn't room for you two—get out!"

"No," Belle said firmly. "We paid for our seats and you can't do this. I'll report you!"

To whom? Nobody knew where they were!

"Lord—" Belle began desperately. Suddenly, with a

screech an old truck pulled up beside them and a Chinese man called, "Get in—quick!"

Jumping into the stranger's truck, they roared off and lost sight of the obnoxious driver. Their new friend drove them right up to the door of the mission house in Kunming. Then came another test of Belle's unselfishness. She was aching for John, aching to get to Tali just as soon as possible. Missionary Dave Harrison, her host, asked, "Will you stay on here and teach my class so I can make a two-week trip into the country and visit some Chinese Christians who need me?"

Two weeks! Belle had always believed that a specific call from God was not always necessary—that the need was the call. Of course she would stay. And as the class of university students grew, she started a second and a third class.

Belle worried over another trip via truck on the Burma Road, but just then a Friends' Ambulance Unit from England offered a ride. Had Belle not stayed the extra two weeks, she would not have made the contact.

Those were the shaky, unpredictable war years, and when Belle did reach Tali she was told John had gone on to Paoshan to assist a Chinese doctor. A letter, however, from Kathryn arrived, the first in seven months, and was full of childish news and chatter. Belle was relieved to know the little girl was content even in captivity.

In the days that followed, this bulletin was issued: "All territory west of Tali is in the military zone. You cannot go any farther. The Salween Canyon is in the front line of battle. Not even American soldiers are allowed there, only Chinese."

What was there to do but pray? Belle spent time alone on her knees, and while she was quiet in God's presence her thoughts had time to straighten out. John got through the military zone because he was with a *Chinese* doctor! *How perfectly marvelously God works,* she thought. He would surely "bring her again" to the Lisu.

She prayed ten days. Nothing happened. Enough was

enough. She took matters into her own hands and walked to the residence of General Song to ask for a travel permit. Because she was so shabbily dressed, the soldiers at the gate only laughed at her.

Belle resorted again to prayer. That same day an officer arrived with a message for her. "The General has phoned your husband and asked him to come here to Tali immediately. He has sent his own car."

Later she learned why. The Japanese in the Salween Canyon were bribing the Lisu to help them across the river. Suddenly this Chinese general realized the importance of soliciting the friendship of the tribes they called "earth people—dirt."

On August 14 John and Belle were reunited (again!) and escorted into General Song's office. "Will you help us win the Lisu over?" the general asked.

John nodded and smiled. "We have already settled it. We told them the Japanese would expect them to renounce Christ. That was enough."

After the war, Belle learned that the Japanese conquered the west bank of the Salween up to the area where the Lisu Christians lived. Beyond that, they received no cooperation.

"Shame on all of us Chinese," the general said later to a body of university students. "Why have we not cared for these tribespeople as the foreign missionaries did?"

But only two groups ever cared enough to live the rugged life of the canyon—missionaries and Communists.

In the days following, Belle floated as if in a dream. They were guests at a banquet in Song's private residence, given a tour of beautiful Lake-of-the-Ear, riding in the general's car, and a military escort with all expenses paid right up the side of the canyon and into Oak Flat Village!

"There was no shepherd, neither did my shepherds search for my flock, but the shepherds fed themselves, and fed not my flock."
—Ezekiel 34:8

"In the light of eternity we shall see that what we desired would have been fatal to us, and that what we would have avoided was essential to our well-being." —Fenelon

"Failure is often God's own tool for carving some of the finest outlines in the character of His children." —T. Hodgkin

A baby bee sealed in its hexagonal cell of wax must fight and struggle and strain to get out. So narrow is the outlet that he rubs off the membrane binding his wings! Now he can fly! Once a blundering person poked open a cell of wax with a pin so the baby bee would have no difficulties. The little bee could not fly and the other bees killed him. He had lost his wing-power.

"Saved from the struggle, but ruined in the process."
—Anonymous

"Tribulation worketh patience . . . experience . . . hope." —Romans 5:3–4

XII.

BUSINESS AS USUAL

1943–1946

Young Peter, the goatherd, squatted by the side of the nanny and managed to wring out one cupful of milk. Bah! Why did Ma-ma give milk to her baby? The Chinese said milk was poisonous. Why didn't little Danny drink milk from his Ma-ma for three years like other babies? Or honey water? Peter just didn't understand the strange ways of white people. And he had forgotten to wash his hands first. Now he guessed Ma-ma would make a fuss about that too!

Well, he was ten years old and big enough to attend the Boys' Bible School next March. He would learn to read and write and maybe preach and let a younger boy herd goats! Then he laughed. He remembered how funny it had been the time Ma-ma and Eva tried to milk the goat. They had pulled and squeezed, pulled and squeezed without getting a drop!

Peter carried the cup of milk to Ma-ma. Yes, as he expected, she put on her worried look. She didn't say it, but the accusation "lazy" was written in her eyes.

Daniel Kreadman Kuhn was born August 1, 1943, with

Irish-red hair and pearly white skin. Cows, canned milk or powdered were non-existent. The nanny goat was the only source of nourishment for the hungry little boy. No doctor had been available, but a CIM nurse, Dorothy Burrows, took her vacation time and visited the Salween Canyon and delivered the baby. She stayed four weeks; then John escorted her down the mountainside and back to Tali. He continued on to Chungking to a superintendents' conference. Charles Peterson and Eva stayed at Oak Flat with Belle.

The very next day, Charles fell sick with rheumatic fever. Next, the girl who did their laundry became ill and could not work. The skies opened up and a torrent of rain poured upon the earth, hour after hour, day after day. Then a runner announced that Colonel Hsie, the Chinese in charge of the Canyon, and his Number Two wife were stopping for a social call. In addition to all these crises, Belle was facing the start of the November RSBS!

Eight months before, the postmaster who lived in the town of Six Treasures, a day's travel away, had deserted his post as the Japanese drew closer. Then Belle's cook announced he was quitting. Still, in spite of living in the danger zone of the war, thirty-six cowherds had attended the Boys' Bible School. To add to the number, the principal of a small school teaching the Chinese language to Lisu children canceled his classes so his forty boys could also attend. Belle was swamped with seventy-six students! That had been eight months ago.

Peter, the goatherd, watched all the calamities with an anxious eye. Would he be expected to work even harder, now that everybody was sick? Curling up on his mat, Peter refused to get up. "I'm sick, too!" he complained as he rubbed his stomach vigorously.

"Oh, God, help!" Belle cried. She assigned Eva to cooking and washing clothes while she prepared a tray of food three times a day and carried it down the muddy path to Charles's hut. Night after night she walked the floor with

Danny, who cried and cried. She was so tired she could hardly stand on her feet. "Shall we cancel RSBS?" she wondered.

Charles, unable to get out of bed because of the pain, said, "Ask Orville Carson at Luda to come help us. He could take care of me, so you wouldn't have to run back and forth."

Orville sent word he would come, but before he arrived Charles's pain grew worse and he asked for a shot of morphine. Belle, who had never learned the mystery of managing a charcoal fire, blew on the coals and stirred them up so she could boil the hypodermic needle and sterilize it. In the teeming rain she slid down the mountainside to his shanty, carrying the small cook pot with its sterile needle, all covered with waterproof plastic.

Belle never before had given anyone a shot and the doubts raged within. Do I stick the needle straight in or lightly under the skin? What if it hits a vein or artery or a bone? What if the needle breaks off? What if I killed him? Oh, God, please help me now!

Charles sat up on one elbow trying not to groan. "Nothing to it," he assured, his eyes blinked hard trying to adjust and concentrate on what he was doing. "Look, just push hard with a jab—like this!" His thumb slipped, the needle shot up and out the open window. It was Belle's only needle.

"Oh, God," she cried again. Nothing to do but try to find that needle. So, struggling up the mountain to her hut, lighting a lantern, and sliding back down in the rain on hands and knees, Belle searched through the mud under the window and finally found the thoroughly contaminated needle. Back up the trail she climbed. By now the charcoal fire was cold. Belle never did remember what happened after that. Perhaps she fainted—or had hysterics. At any rate, Eva returned home from a meeting and took things into her capable hands.

Colonel Hsie eventually arrived, took over Belle's "clinic house" and installed his girlfriend permanantly at Oak Flat for her safety, since he expected the Japanese to storm the Salween Canyon any day.

Colicky Danny still cried all night long because of the goat's milk, and there was nothing Belle could do to relieve him. Only Eva could soothe him asleep by heating the milk and wrapping him warmly in a blanket. "God, my King, command deliverance," Belle prayed night after night. And He answered! Soon John returned and together they shared the load.

By the end of 1943, the Japanese occupied part of the Canyon directly across the river from Belle. As she and John watched, they saw the town of Luchang burn to the ground under the enemy's torch. Once again a big decision faced them, a decision now involving the safety of many people's lives. Shall they cancel the Girls' Bible School?

After praying, Belle decided not to cancel the Bible school. This would have a stabilizing effect on the Lisu. They would see that God was still in control. By now Charles Peterson had left for a much needed three-month rest. When the Bible school opened, twenty-five bright and eager girls arrived in spite of the war being at their very doorstep. Belle, John and baby Danny all suffered from influenza during this school session.

One young man who attended RSBS had been nicknamed Romeo, before the death of his young wife. Belle heard that he had returned to his village after only one month of study and taught the people each night and even built a small mud chapel. The month Danny was born Belle did not teach but the students visited her and once they spent a night in prayer.

Belle noticed a grossly running sore on Romeo's neck and knew at once that TB had recurred. The CIM now had a hospital in Tali and Belle told Romeo he could go there to be healed and they would not charge him one penny.

Romeo was not ecstatic as Belle expected; he merely thanked her. Then he said, "No, I don't think I will go."

Belle argued with him. "It would mean healing!"

"I know my sickness is made worse by lack of good food. If I lived in a city and stayed near white people, I would be better in body. But Ma-ma, where would I get food for my soul like I get here?"

Even knowing the Lisu were terrified of his illness, that he was repulsive to some of them, Romeo stayed on in his village and taught all who would listen. People from the wicked Village-of-Wheat-Level also listened to Romeo, and soon a prayer group formed. A few months later Romeo, who had chosen a closer walk with God rather than healing of the body, died of his disease.

Another of Belle's students, Chi-lee, almost convinced her that a *missionary* had discovered the missing link. He fit the descriptions anthropologists usually give: low forehead, wild, untamed hair, a perplexed look, large jaw, dirty, full of fleas and the itch. Yet he could read and write! (Then he couldn't be the missing link, Belle thought with relief.)

Chi-lee was a Christian, but he could not pass his exams. He was from a mountain ravine higher up, which Belle named "The Heathen Patch," for no missionary over the years was able to enter it to make a spiritual impact. Chi-lee wasn't a bit discouraged that he hadn't passed. He was content to just listen, and after a bath and a haircut and some of Ma-ma's magic salve, he felt so much better!

He went back to his village full of hope that he would win his family to the Lord, but the villagers burned his house down and his own father refused him shelter.

Undaunted, Chi-lee began to teach the youth of the village, but the elders rose up against him in fear of the demons. "Stop teaching or we will surely kill you!" they sternly warned.

He then built a lean-to of branches deep in the woods, caught malaria carried by mosquitos and died—alone.

Why did God take him, the Christian witness for those two villages? Belle wondered. *Why?* When farther on was another area where thousands of unreached Lisu lived, Lisu who ten years previous had sent out a delegation to ask an elderly Christian woman to send them a teacher so they might believe? Ten years ago! And the sixty-year-old woman was still trying to find one Christian who would go! Chi-lee might have been the one.

Belle was completely alone when the Boys' Bible School started, this time with no pencils, paper or ink. "Lord, how can we possibly hold a school session?" Belle prayed as she looked at her scanty supplies on her desk. The Lisu church volunteered two evangelists, Thomas Hemp and Luke Fish, for the month of March. When opening day arrived, Teacher Thomas did not show up, no students from the West Bank came, and there were still no writing supplies.

Belle learned that a Communist spy had set himself up on the West Bank to recruit Lisu youth for the military, concentrating on the Christian ones, refusing them passes across the Salween. *Will harassments never end?* Belle pondered. By now she had proven by experience that God can work when man cannot. So she prayed.

How did God answer? He sent *American* soldiers right to her door. (Due to censorship she could not explain in detail.) She fed them well, much to their appreciation. In return, they asked, "Is there anything we can do for you, Mrs. Kuhn?" So Belle explained her situation. They made the arrangements and on the fifth day of school, teacher Thomas walked in with three pupils, plus the writing supplies and Charles Peterson.

When classes were over, Lisu teacher Luke wrote a new song, Lucius designed a certificate, and Bible school ended in jubilation.

In 1944, RSBS was held as usual. General Stillwell cut the Japanese supply line, and peace and quiet returned to the canyon. In September furlough time was near, and the most wonderful news of all arrived. Kathryn was rescued along with many others on the mercy ship *Gripsholm*, and was already safe in America and waiting to see Mummy, Daddy, and her baby brother whom she had not met.

Down the Canyon side went the Kuhns. The days of

truck travel were exhausting. In October they arrived in India after catching a flight out of China. Then they were shifted on to Calcutta and Bombay, classed as "refugees," and jammed onto a troop ship with an unknown destination.

Women and men were separated. John bunked in the hold, and Belle and Danny stayed in a cabin with ten other women (John was allowed to see his family only two hours a day.) There were no portholes for fresh air, the quarters were cramped, and a movie blared continually just outside their door. Cooped up for thirty-six days with lively Danny, now one and a half years old, in the stifling, nerve-wracking conditions, wore Belle to exhaustion. Everyone, regardless of age, was served an enormous plate of he-man food— steaks, French fries, corn, biscuits, and pie. Danny was often sick and after two weeks of life on board ship during wartime, Belle felt near the breaking point.

Civilians were not allowed on deck. Dangers were everywhere. The ship had no railings and holes through which the cables passed were left uncovered. "Lord, help!" Belle cried one day, as they lined up for a meal. Danny was so heavy in her arms, she could hardly hold him. The captain, much annoyed at being burdened with "refugees" during the serious business of winning a war, had warned them all: "If a kid falls overboard, we don't stop!"

That day standing in line, Belle really felt she would faint, when suddenly a motherly-type woman took Danny from her arms and said, "From now on I'll help you with this big boy. I'll wash him, carry him back and forth to meals, and keep an eye on him." Belle considered her an angel from God.

The ship docked in California. The Kuhns were met by the Red Cross, who fed them and drove them right to the door of the CIM. After a brief rest they took a train to Philadelphia where Kathryn was staying. John and Belle could hardly believe this was their Kathryn, a teenager almost as tall as her parents. They were a completed family again.

After six months of living with the kind Harrisons, Belle's nerves still could not unwind. She prayed for a place of their own—such an impossible, almost unreasonable request in wartime.

At this time John was told that some shares of stock in a company that his father had left him had matured into $6,000! John decided to take a course at a theological seminary in Dallas, Texas. They would need a two-bedroom house, with a fenced-in yard for Danny, near the seminary for John and near a high school for Kathryn.

"Oh, if only I could sleep . . . and sleep . . . and sleep," Belle confided to the Lord. "In our own home, I could do just that."

She took the next train to Dallas. Real estate people there just laughed at her ideas of finding such a house—or any house, during the critical national housing shortage! Building materials were needed for the war, married servicemen got priority. In fact, the day she arrived and asked for a room in the YWCA, the girl at the desk just stared at her. "Are you naive? Where have you been? There's a war on. You won't get a room *anywhere* in this city."

"I need a room for a month," Belle said timidly. "Could you try, please?"

"I phoned nine hotels this morning to place another woman, and *nobody* had a room! Well, wait a minute, I'll try."

On the fourth phone call she found Belle a room in a third-class, run-down hotel in a bad section of town.

"Do you know how lucky you are?" The real estate agent greeted her the next morning. "We have only one house to offer, 1718 Ripley Street, near a high school and Dallas Theological Seminary." He went on to describe Belle's dream house. It was owned by Christians, had everything they had prayed for, and the sale price was $4,500!

Only three days after her conversation with the YWCA secretary, Belle owned a house, had paid for it and signed the deed. Her sense of humor returned, and she couldn't resist going back to the YWCA to tell the girl what happened.

The young lady almost passed out. She staggered back, grasped for a chair and collapsed into it. "You've renewed my faith in God," she said, almost speechless.

Belle had her first real vacation in years as she happily shopped for secondhand furniture, a piano, and everything else she needed. Once in her own home, Belle was able to catch up on her rest and soon felt better than she had in years.

The fall of the atom bomb abruptly ending the war with Japan cut short their year's furlough. China was once again open to missionaries. The CIM asked all superintendents to return one year ahead of their families, meaning another separation for John and Belle. "God first" was their marriage motto. John sailed January 1946.

Belle stayed on in their house for a year with the two children. When time came to sell the house, she asked $6,100 and sold it to the first person who came along. That meant they had lived rent-free in their own home for two years, and had gained financially, as well as every other way. With nerves relaxed and rested, she was ready again for Canyon life.

"Perils of water,
Perils of robbers,
Perils by mine own countrymen,
Perils by the heathen,
Perils in the city,
Perils in the wilderness,
Perils in the sea,
Perils among false brethren."
—2 Corinthians 11:26

"Out of this nettle, Danger,
We pluck this flower, Safety."
—Katherine Mansfield

"God hath not given us the spirit of fear." —2 Timothy 1:7

"A foul fiend came over the hill to meet him. Should he flee or stand his ground? But he remembered—he had no armour for his back." —Pilgrim's Progress

As the nightingales sing sweetest when farthest from their nests, so Wilfrid did the best service for Christianity when farthest from home. —Wilfrid, c. 680

"Be Thou my strong habitation, whereunto I may continually resort." —Psalm 71:3

"And, lo, I am with you always, even unto the end of the world." —Matthew 28:20

XIII.

ESCAPE OVER THE HUMP

1947–1950

Three-year-old Danny never knew what would happen next on this adventure with his lively and unpredictable mom. The train left Philadelphia and traveled its steely way down to Houston, Texas. Watching everything from the observation car was fun as they rambled through state after state, down through beautiful Appalachia, Tennessee, deep into Mississippi, Louisiana and flat, spacious Texas.

A small freighter, the *Joseph Lee*, with ancient boilers, carrying cotton and kerosene, was docked in Houston. It was the only ship available. The longshoremen were on strike. The freighter lacked railings and would take forty-six days to reach Shanghai. "Slow boat to China" could not have described it better.

How exciting it was for Danny to stand on board, held tightly by Mom, and look all around as the ship started out, fifty miles down a channel and into the Gulf of Mexico. A missionary teacher on board held Sunday school every single day, telling the finest stories and playing great games! Crossing didn't seem long to Danny, for he could think up more mischief faster than his mother could think up solutions.

They exercised every day, watching the billowy waves from a safe distance.

Pulling into the big, bustling Shanghai port, Danny looked in vain for the daddy he hadn't seen in over a year. John, however, was still touring Yunnan Province and the tribal areas. So the CIM house sheltered them from the bitterly cold Chinese winter.

When John returned, he described the wartime devastation throughout China. "Bridges everywhere are blown up, roads destroyed, robbers making the most of the opportunity."

Belle and Danny flew to sunny Yunnan in a Flying Fortress, while John and a friend drove a truck loaded with their supplies and belongings. From Kunming to Paoshan, Belle and Danny rode the truck driven by John on the wartorn Burma Road. The clumsy war truck felt like the *inside* of a butterchurn.

At Tali they were reunited with Eva Tseng, who was now in nurses' training.

"Oh, Ma-ma, let me quit school and go back with you to Lisuland! I'll give up everything just to be with you. I could cook and mind Danny . . ."

Belle was tempted, but she had learned that even affections must be crucified. "No," she said firmly, "you will graduate in one and a half years. I can't let you stop your schooling."

"What if Danny falls sick?"

Belle didn't budge. "I'll trust God for Danny."

Belle and Danny started into the canyon to Lisuland while John stayed behind in Paoshan, trying to find housing for a missionary couple. Lucius escorted them, and Chinese coolies carried the luggage.

The land along the Salween River seemed beautiful on the surface—peacocks with eye-jarring plumage, leopards drinking at the water's edge, monkeys loudly spreading false rumors—but the valley was full of malignant malaria. "The worst malaria spot in the world," once declared a 1942 issue of Time Magazine.

Within the canyon was Wu-ti-ho, the "River Without a Bottom," the natives named it. Deep into the jungle lived pythons with jaws that unhinged and gulped down large live hogs. In the Salween River, big fish with skin hard as leather opened and shut mouths shaped like folding doors.

Danny rode in a mountain chair, but when they reached the last 2,000-foot climb, the Lisu met them. What a surprise for Danny! A beautiful, sure-footed horse trimmed in silver bells with an embroidered blanket on its back and two Lisu guards by his side to lead the horse and wait on him.

Enthroned like a little king—the world beneath his feet, adventure lurking around every twist of the road—Danny shouted for joy!

The Christian Lisu took the loads from the coolies and laid them on their own backs, promising the coolies a feast of roasted pork. "Sure, sure," grumbled the coolies. "These Lisu lie. Small chance of a feast up here in this terrible country. Maybe they'll kill and eat *us*!" That wasn't an idle comment. It sometimes happened.

Up the side of the canyon the party went, winding around and around, like toiling up the sides of a lighthouse.

"My horse has bells!" Danny sang gaily. "My horse bumps me all over the place!"

The coolies were astonished at the change in the ferocious Lisu who had become Christians, the affectionate and generous people they had always called "dirt." When God finished making all people, their legend ran, He scraped the dirt from His feet and from it made the Lisu.

Belle and Danny slept in a cornbin one night, a hayloft another night, while typhus-carrying fleas feasted upon them. *What a change from the comfortable home in Dallas*, Belle thought, *but I wouldn't want to be anywhere else in the world*.

Arriving at Oak Flat, they discovered that the old home had given up, sighed and fallen in upon itself. Two Christian Lisu, Pade-John and his wife Ruth, welcomed them with cold, pure water to drink, and hot water for washing. They took up shelter in their old shanty, but no sooner were they settled than the rain poured down—the first rain in six months. All the welcome-home gifts were in the form of eggs (more than eight dozen), as the drought had burned up most vegetable crops.

The first Sunday, three hundred Lisu came from all over the canyon to greet Ma-ma and Danny. Most of the Kuhns' personal things had been taken from the shanty, and Belle suspected Pade-John had helped himself.

The village was spell-bound over Danny and his toy wind-up train, which shot sparks and tinkled a bell. The Lisu sat by the hour watching it and one of Kathryn's old dolls, which opened and shut eyes and cried, "Ma-ma."

Before the RSBS began, John was home. At that session they taught more students than ever before. Belle introduced the Lisu evangelists to modern ways of presenting the gospel to children.

When RSBS was over, John left on another trip.

One night Belle awoke to hear Danny babbling nonsense, out of his head with fever and covered with red spots. He was too weak to even sit up.

"Oh, God—typhus—those fleas!" Belle cried silently. She was the only white person in the canyon and many days from medical help.

If only I had taken nurse Eva with me, her thoughts tormented her. *If only I had left Danny in America, if only . . .*

She was not trained in medicine and had only simple remedies with her. Night after night she sat by Danny's bed, cooling the fever, singing and praying, trying to coax nourishment between his cracked lips. Besides that, the Lisu church, which had backslidden during her absence, brought all their problems to her. They seemed too discouraged and weak to take on any leadership.

It was a pale and listless little boy who survived typhus, but he did survive.

The first indication that God wanted the Kuhns out of

Oak Flat occurred when Belle was alone one night and heard two men under her window using bird chirps to signal each other. One on each side of her shanty, which had open windows and no locks, the men drew closer and closer. Belle slipped noiselessy from bed, crossed the room to sit beside sleeping Danny. *Missionaries do get martyred.* The thought chilled her. "Lord, is it to happen to me?"

The bird calls ceased and after crouching in the dark another hour, Belle lay down to sleep.

After that, one of the elders in the church slept at her house with a loaded gun until John returned. "Once we were welcomed and loved by all," Belle mourned. "What has happened to the church? Was it the war? Communist propaganda against us? The fact that the Lisu church lacked a white teacher and missionary during those years?"

A short time after this a man named Keh and his profligate son made a visit to Belle late one night to threaten her. Keh wanted his son appointed schoolteacher in the Christian school and Belle had refused. Fortunately, a Christian farmer named Chu followed the man into Belle's kitchen and quietly sat in a corner as a witness. Keh's blackmail plot failed, and an upstanding Christian Lisu was given the job.

Belle knew she now had personal enemies—in addition to Dai, a Chinese who led a group of Communist brigands and had vowed to "get" Belle.

The climax of the persecution directed against her came when Keh, the village magistrate representing Chinese law, tied two prisoners against the wall of her tiny kitchen where she had to see them day after day. You don't dare to interfere with Chinese justice," he challenged her. "I could bring a lawsuit against you."

John was home at the time, so Keh approached him. Keh was willing to release the prisoners if John would sign a letter recommending his friend, Pade-John, as pastor over all the Lisu churches in that area. Pade-John was a backslider, and John refused.

On the last day of RSBS, crowds of Christians gathered.

Keh also showed up, leading a crowd of farmers. An elderly Christian man, Ah-be-pa, had cut the prisoners loose and he himself was seized by the angry mob. The Christian Lisu squared-off to defend their old deacon.

"Stop!" John ordered as he stepped between the two angry groups. To avoid bloodshed he signed the paper.

Back in the hut, he sat with his head bowed while Lucius explained to Belle. "Ma-pa had to do it. What would the heathen say if they heard there was a big fight among the Christians? Keh and Pade-John still consider themselves God's children. Nobody will believe the paper and nobody wants Pade-John for pastor!"

The only real victories are spiritual victories, and the only real defeats are spiritual defeats.

"And Keh had to pick closing day to do this," Belle wept. "We worked so hard here for thirteen years and we end up with a divided, backslidden, quarreling church, a church that almost came to blows and bloodshed! I'll never dare live here alone with Keh and Pade-John and Dai as enemies."

So the Kuhns moved from Oak Flat across the Salween River to Village of Olives in December 1948. Lucius and his friends built them a house right next to his own. Hundreds of Christian Lisu let their buckwheat crop wait while they worked on the house. One very poor family gave forty days free labor. Besides hauling logs to construct the house, one hundred fifty other Lisu carried the Kuhns' possessions down the mountain and over the river. The Lisu also built a dormitory for the RSBS big enough for one hundred students.

There was a time in Belle's early life when she dreamed of becoming a dean of women and helping students, a dream of teaching the magnificent English literature. Did she regret coming to the Lisu? Never. As she watched her spiritual sons and daughters building her a home, she thanked God for leading her here, to the end of the earth. "May I be worthy of *them*" was her prayer.

Four months after they moved to the west bank of the river, Dai and his Communist band attacked Oak Flat Village, looking especially for Belle. Keh joined the search, and when they couldn't find Belle, they made plans to cross the river and hunt her down.

Belle always remembered the end of this month as "Bloody Christmas." Dai and Keh were holding a young laird at Place-of-Action Village as prisoner. On Christmas Eve the laird's friends came to his rescue and dropped hand granades down upon Dai's sleeping men. Thirteen men were blown to pieces and others horribly injured. The twenty-three-year-old laird escaped and announced his intention of moving over with his household of seventy to live near Ma-ma.

"Oh, no," Belle groaned. "That will draw the attention of the Communists to us, for the Communists will surely try to avenge that massacre."

The laird, called "Grandpa," moved over to Olives, and for a while the villagers were kept busy ferrying over his loot, then cutting all the rope bridges but one to protect him, guarding him and running his errands.

Another event occurred that year. Chungking had fallen to the Communists. Because of this, many had a premonition that all of China would soon be under Communist rule. In December, Belle opened a small note given to her by a runner. "Red Thomas," a Communist who led a band of *lo-zi-lo-pa* (robbers), but one who knew and respected Belle, was on his way to "liberate" Village of Olives. He promised protection to Ma-ma.

"Shall I run?" Belle wondered. "Oh, dear Lord, do guide me." She read Mal. 3:17–18 that morning: "My jewels . . . I will spare them."

A second note came from Red Thomas, a very courteous and humble note. But Belle knew he would fight the laird living among them. She prepared to be in the center of a battle—by much prayer and hiding some of the medicines and kerosene so all would not be confiscated.

False alarm! Only three gunshots reverberated up and down the canyon, and in the morning life was normal again. Two days later Red Thomas arrived peaceably, chagrined to find the wily laird had escaped from his trap.

Then to the surprise of all the laird returned, announcing that he had a change of heart, and thought communism was a very good thing. In fact, he and his men submitted voluntarily to Red Thomas and called themselves loyal Communists. Red Thomas, on the other hand, declared he was still a Christian!

Belle's first impulse was to laugh at the turn of events, but the situation was really too serious for smiles. Neither man fully understood all the implications of communism. They had just heard of the fall of Chungking and wanted to be on the winning side!

Paoshan was besieged all around by brigands and John was trapped there for two months. Belle narrowly missed being captured by Dai and his men, who were only a few hours away. "Ma-ma, haven't you heard? Dai was shot by the laird's followers," she was told. That was the one time Belle sighed with relief at a death.

Bandits were always used by the Communists to upset any area they wished to take. Then, when crime was on the upsurge and things out of control, the Communists "liberated" the poor, grateful people.

With John away, and the dead Dai's men still alive and so close that April, Belle did have reason to worry. Would Dai's men cross the river and come after her?

"Mommy, listen to the plóp-plop-plop on the pumpkin leaves!" Danny shouted one morning from the loft where he slept.

Belle jumped out of bed and ran to the window. Rain! In the dry season! How could such a thing happen? And why?

Rain fell like a torrent for two solid weeks, turning the river and its branching streams into foaming floods. Dai's men could not reach them now.

The day before, Belle had been given a note from John by a robber who made the long trip up to Olives for that purpose! The robber had a little sister in Paoshan who was a Christian. She suggested that John write to Belle, then begged her brother to deliver the note. "Am having a wonderful time witnessing," John wrote.

By January 1950, John finally came home, bringing Eva, now an R.N. He also brought hundreds of Lisu Catechisms. For some time Belle knew she must get Danny back to civilization. He was six years old, needing formal schooling and playmates. One day Danny came indoors and sat down, his face very solemn.

"Mummy, I'm not going to heaven."

"Why not?"

His eyes filled with tears. "If you want me to be a Christian, don't let me go outside anymore." Belle understood. In Olives they had no fenced yard, and heathen children of all ages and types came to play with Danny. He was picking up their filthy language and habits, not in practice but into his ears and eyes and mind.

The only way out of the Canyon and China would be up "over the hump," the 11,000-foot-high Pien Ma Pass. Kunming was bombed daily and it was impossible to go that way. Cities and villages at the base of the mountain had been seized by Communists. How long before the Kuhns would be imprisoned—or worse? Communism would never allow Christianity to thrive under its rule.

Belle and Danny left home March 10, with Lisu guides and began to climb. The last sign of human life was a log cabin of a native; then they were in desolate terrain. From 7:30 A.M. to 7:00 P.M. they climbed, not daring to stop five minutes for food.

A party of men had crossed over into China from the Burma side, and Belle's only hope lay in following their tracks. By noon, snow and sleet beat down on them, almost obliterating the tracks. Belle rode the mule and Danny was carried in a mountain chair, singing at the top of his lungs. He was warm and dry, but Belle's boots were filled with ice water, numbing her legs to the knees. Words of another mountaineer came to mind: "Climb or die." There was no turning back, even though the Lisu were afraid to go on.

Eleven thousand feet up, they could look down into Burma and it was just as dark and stormy. By now one Lisu was carrying Danny piggyback. The mule slid into a snow-bank and Belle was obliged to walk, willing one foot in front of the other. But they were out of Communist China.

That night they slept in wet bedding, but God prevented Belle's rheumatism from recurring. For days they pushed on through the downpour of freezing rain, finally arriving at Myitkyina, the most important city in Upper Burma, half a world away from America.

"Give me the mountains where the giants live!" —Caleb, age 85, Joshua 14:12

"Doubt sees the obstacles . . ." —Anonymous

Belle often noticed that when a missionary came into a native home, the evil spirits departed. Other missionaries confirmed this. The presence of a Christian was a hindrance. "Dagon was fallen upon his face to the ground before the ark of the Lord." —1 Samuel 5:4

"He that paid his taxes from a fish's mouth will supply all my needs." —Robert M. McCheyne

Poor in this world's goods, rich in faith.

"I live for my beautiful home and garden. I have filled the house with everything money can buy." —A friend in America to Belle

"Will there be any stars?
Any stars in my crown?" —An old hymn

"No pain, no palm. No cross, no crown. No thorn, no throne. No gall, no glory. Learn to glory in tribulations. This is the only world where you can give God that glory." —Robert M. McCheyne

XIV

THAILAND

1951–1954

"Not too much curry this time!" Belle knew enough of the Thai language to converse with the pretty thirty-year-old Christian woman who lived with them as cook, seamstress and housekeeper. Belle had chosen the nickname "Madame Curry" after sampling the food. Tongue-scorching yellow rice! Spicy condiments! Meat, fiery with curry!

Madame Curry smiled, head tipped to one side. As soon as Belle's back was turned, she dropped another scoopful of curry into the pot. Married to a former Buddhist priest, proud of her three children, Madame Curry was always willing and able to stretch a meal for all the unexpected guests to the mission station. Chop the meat chunks smaller, mix them with vegetables, water the sauce, fluff up the rice, and a meal planned for six accommodated ten! And always plenty of hot tea.

In January 1951, the CIM, eighty years old, had ordered the evacuation of all missionaries from Communist China. Churches were forced to close. Native pastors, some of them educated, scholarly men, were put to work cleaning streets or shoveling manure on farms. The Cultural Revolution had begun!

To stay would endanger the Chinese Christians. Six hundred and one adults and 284 children, not counting many who had already reached Hong Kong, were withdrawn from China. John Kuhn escaped in July 1951.

The CIM organized the OMF (Overseas Missionary Fellowship) to reach the mountain tribes of Burma, Indochina and Thailand. In North Thailand a Lisu tribe of 5,000 was completely unreached by the gospel. Missionaries had been in Thailand more than 100 years, but never reached past the Thai people to the aborigines of the mountains. Belle learned that the same Communist government which forced missionaries out of China also inspired many tribes to leave China and settle in peaceful Thailand.

"Start climbing again?" Belle said to herself, as she thought about the new missionary venture. "I'm fifty years old. I'm *tired*! I want to sit in a rocking chair on a porch somewhere and just have time to think. I want to be with my children. My bones ache and my nerves never did get fully rested up."

"You must take it easy now, you deserve it, you need it, you earned it," said a stranger to the knight in gold armor. The giver of that advice proved to be a villain named Self. God began to speak to her through a child's book she was reading to Danny.

Taking it easy would mean slow decay. She felt the Lord's nudging.

Lord, are you asking me to do the impossible—again?

Of course there are younger, smarter missionaries coming along; healthier, full of enthusiasm and faith and courage. But they lack experience!

Oh dear, why couldn't she ever win an argument with the Lord?

Do you really choose ease? He asked her.

No, Lord, no! But will I have to learn another language? Just a little bit of Thai. He seemed to encourage her.

Lord, I do want Your will. In fact, I accept it with both hands as good and perfect for me.

So it came to pass that in July 1952, Belle left Wheaton, Illinois, after spending two years in America. Kathryn graduated from college and entered Multnomah School of the Bible in Portland, Oregon. Danny was placed in the Aldrich home there along with the nine Aldrich children.

Belle and John sailed from New York City on the French ship *Liberte*, stopping for meetings and conventions at England, Holland, France and Switzerland. Then on to Singapore.

At Singapore they boarded another ship for Thailand, to the mouth of the Chao Phraya River. Up the river their boat crept, past cargo crafts, rows of coconut trees, steaming jungle—twenty miles in all. Past little villages of teakwood houses on high stilts along the river. The jungle meandered down to the river edge and separated into many little clearings. The Kuhns arrived in the city of Bangkok, October 6, 1952.

Leaving the city behind, they rode by train to Chiengmai, North Thailand, the base camp for the OMF, a home-away-from-home for all workers, a haven for rest and spiritual refueling. Chiengmai city, once capital of the old Kingdom of Laos, sat at the very end of the railroad line, and from there good roads led into the mountains.

John was superintendent of this tribal area, and Belle was a highly organized hostess who kept housekeeping simple, oversaw Thai servants who laundered and cooked. Though always cheerful outwardly, she once confided to a friend that she fought mental depression all her life, day by day, asking God to deliver her. Her prayer life, a habit begun in MBI days, started at 5:30 A.M. Though hostess, it was understood she could also trek into out-lying villages to teach and give medical aid. She found the Chinese language could be used for some of the Thai tribes.

Thailand was civilized, with schools even in the villages,

and in Bangkok, universities and hospitals. The country was also very religious; godless Buddhism was firmly rooted.

Belle sat down one day and made some notes. "I'm going to think of our work here as the challenge of a high mountain. We are standing at the base—Chiengmai. Once we get things organized here we could turn Base Camp over to another missionary and try to establish an Advance Camp up in the mountains among the tribes. New missionaries coming to us could get a taste of primitive living there. Then—Summit Camp would be established when a group of native Christians ask for a teacher and offer to build him a house. After that, the sooner the new little churches become indigenous, the better, with a native pastor and deacons."

Home for Belle was now an eight-bedroom house in the middle of an orchard edging a riverbank, with a sandy beach. In the marketplace she often saw Lisu and Miao tribespeople bargaining for bright blankets, canned sardines, silver belts, and cook pots.

"A li kwa je lo?" (Where are you going?)

The Lisu stared in unbelief. A white "auntie" speaking Lisu, with such a funny accent!

Belle kept on praying for the unreached Lisu. A short time later, missionaries Orville and Hazel Carlson took over the running of Base Camp in Chiengmai so John and Belle could visit the Lisu tribes, joining a party of four other missionaries. The first day they hiked across the plains and stopped at a village at the base of the mountains. The second day they began to climb, over fallen branches and rooted-up trees (for a hurricane had passed through earlier), skirting deep ravines.

Six hours later they stopped to eat and spend the night. Belle crawled into a sleeping bag placed on mud for a mattress, pulled mosquito netting over her face and tried to sleep.

The next day they followed a path that doubled back and forth on itself like a coiled rope. Twenty times in a half hour they crossed the same icy cold mountain stream. It was impossible to wade barefoot. Razor-sharp rocks lined the bottom. Belle walked through with her shoes on, and soon her wet feet blistered and peeled.

The third day they crossed fields of grain, and Belle stopped to talk to a farmer of the Lahu tribe who spoke Lisu.

"Do you know Wu-sa (God) and that He loves you? Someday He will judge sin, but Jesus can save you."

A pitifully short message, but the others were out of sight over a hill and Belle had to run to catch up. The farmer's reply haunted her: "There is nobody to tell me about Him."

That night in a valley the missionary team played gospel records on a portable phonograph machine while the people listened politely. They returned to Base Camp the next day, determined more than ever to reach the Lisu.

Six different denominations were laboring in Chiengmai, and Belle was not one to build on other people's foundations. She longed to be in the thick of the spiritual fight. She never did learn enough Thai for more than family prayers and giving instructions to the servants, but among the Lisu, even with its four dialects, she was very proficient.

Belle's first chance to visit the Lisu in North Thailand for a week came when she and another missionary, Edna McLaren, planned a trip to the Lisu village of Ta-Ngo, which had asked for teachers. Ta-Ngo was spread over three mountain ridges, and Headman Honey lived on Ridge Two. The headman of an area was a powerful figure who bound the families together in fear and in economic dependence.

Through rice fields and past Lao villages they started, then up the trail, two white women and three Thai carriers. Up rises and down dips, up, down, and four hours later they were in Ta-Ngo, on Ridge One.

"Here is a white auntie," Belle heard a woman say. They were among the Lisu, but no one welcomed them or offered a place to sleep. Ridge Two was across a ravine eighty-feet deep, so on they walked until they found a deserted shanty stable with earth floor. Belle and Edna were both shaking from nervous exhaustion. Sometimes the trail had almost dead-ended in space. Every time they climbed up a cliff there was a dip of another cliff behind it.

As they unrolled sleeping bags, and while the porters gathered wood, people strolled by, stopping to stare.

"We are teachers who bring you the way of salvation," Belle said.

A twenty-year-old fellow called out, "Yes, I have heard of Jesus. Someday I will believe in Him. My name is Wood Six and my family lives on that ridge. Will you come and preach to us?"

"Of course. Why not believe in our Lord Jesus right now?"

"No, someday."

Just before the sun set the other villagers returned from the fields with their cattle. "Play the phonograph," called a man who had heard it before.

Belle shook her head. The people of Ta-Ngo had often heard gospel records from another missionary, and this time she wanted to teach them songs. The stirring words of "Men of the Household, Repent!" sounded out into the fast-falling night and brought tears to the eyes of some.

Next day Belle took the initiative in reaching the women who were shy and not talkative. She bargained for a polished teakwood crossbow for Danny. No Lisu could resist a bargaining match. She bought a fine bow for ten *baht* from a young boy. His sisters were sitting on their porch sewing, smiling at Belle.

"Are you making your New Year's dresses?" Belle asked. Chinese New Year's Day was not far off when the villagers would drink and dance and sacrifice to devils.

"Come up and see," the girl offered, and Belle scrambled like a monkey up a notched pole.

One of the girls touched her bare arm. "So white, so beautiful."

"I know something more beautiful," said Belle. "A white heart, a clean heart." And she told the story of Jesus' love.

The girls changed the subject, but a seed had been planted in their minds. After a lunch of boiled noodles, Belle and Edna hiked over to Third Ridge and spoke to the women sitting on their porches, sewing. Two men approached, whom Belle mentally named Old Sly and Big Ear.

"Is this your daughter?" said Old Sly, pointing to Edna. "Is she married?"

"No, she is one of God's teachers."

"Sell her to me for a thousand dollars."

Belle explained why he could not have Edna for a second wife. Their lives were soon threatened as the town rowdies appeared and pushed against them. Belle saved the situation by passing around snapshots of the Lisu of Oak Flat.

The next day Belle and Edna treated a sick baby, and the shanty was quickly filled with visitors who watched to see if the white woman would dance and cast spells. Belle fed the baby canned milk with an eye dropper, then seized the opportunity to preach.

A twenty-four-year-old man nicknamed "Taddi" lay in a corner sucking away at his opium pipe. "I will believe someday," he said, "after I break the opium habit."

A little later he called Belle aside. "If you pay me five dollars a family, I will help you convert fifteen families."

"We don't pay anyone for believing. We are not gaining by it."

A week after Belle and Edna returned to Ta-Ngo, they heard that a family named Wood wanted to become Christians. (Natives were given Anglicized names since the original names often had vile meanings.) Allan and Evelyn Crane hired horses and started out for the village.

Belle waited a week, then she and Edna decided to go to Ta-Ngo. (John was still traveling in Miao territory.) They took a bus to Advance Camp Hweiphai and met the Cranes coming back.

"The Wood family burned the demons' altar!" reported

the Cranes. That morning Belle had read from Exodus 34, and verse 13 stood out: "Ye shall destroy their altars."

Belle and Edna lost no time in climbing to Ta-Ngo and asking for Father Wood. If they expected to find a Saul of Tarsus turned Paul, they must have been horribly disappointed. Father Wood lived in a bamboo shanty. An old, dirty opium sot, he was so crippled with arthritis he could not walk. Of his nine children, seven died, even though sacrifices were made to demons, robbing the family of pigs, their flock of chickens, their plowing ox. Now they were poor.

The morning Father Wood decided to cast down the altar and serve God, most of the villagers tried to crowd into the shanty. Father Wood needed no human being to teach him to pray. He talked to God naturally and lovingly, using the most eloquent and poetic Lisu. Then he turned to the demon shelf and shook his fist. "Get out of my life and home," he shouted. "We served you for years and you let my seven children die. Now we belong to God and the Lord Jesus Christ. Be gone!"

He directed his wife and son, Wu-be, to pull down the shelf and it was burned outside while all the people watched in awe, expecting instant punishment from the demons.

When Belle met Father Wood, he was still unwashed and covered with soot, and his wife swollen with beri-beri.

The neighbors whispered behind their hands, "The white people will steal our children. They use the eyes to make medicine."

Belle sat by Father Wood's fire late into the night, explaining some of the great doctrines of the Bible. This first convert from among the Lisu in North Thailand decided he wanted to read, a thing unheard of for a middle-aged fifty-three-year-old tribesman.

Belle put him on vitamins, aspirin for pain, and Atebrin, prophylactically, for malaria, which was always present among Lisu. She also explained cleanliness, and Father Wood actually consented to washing the accumulated grime of a lifetime from his hands.

At the end of a week, the missionaries were eating lunch in the doorway of their hut when Belle suddenly jumped to her feet, amazed. "Look, Edna! Am I seeing visions?" Father Wood, the helpless cripple, was strolling around his hut, gathering firewood!

That night the rain belched down, the roof leaked, and Belle and Edna huddled under sheets of plastic with baskets over their heads. "Oh dear, if I get lumbago again," Belle mourned to herself, "I will never get back down the mountain to Chiengmai, I'll never see John again, I'll never—" She caught herself just in time before self-pity took over.

In a few days the weather cleared and who should come loping up the trail but John, thirty pounds lighter!

Belle and Edna returned with him to Chiengmai but promised the Lisu to return in three weeks.

This time they were given a hut especially for them by order of Headman Honey, who in return asked that the village children be vaccinated against smallpox. True, it wasn't Buckingham Palace! Belle took one look and dubbed it Higgledy-Piggledy House. Their cookstove was three stones. Rolled-up bedding became a chair by day.

Though Father Wood spoke five tribal languages, he was very slow in learning to read—and he turned grumpy when his knee pained. Sunday services were begun in his home.

In February 1954, Edna and nurse Eileen O'Rourke moved into Ta-Ngo and declared it a Summit Camp.

Since John was superintendent of all of West Yunnan, Belle was able to visit other tribes. She met the first Christian of the Yao Tribe, the headman himself.

Veteran missionaries shut out from China arrived to help the Kuhns, and Belle was set free to pioneer again. Soon other Advance and Summit Camps were established over the mountains of North Thailand, not only among Lisu, but among White Miao, Blue Miao, Lahu, Akha. Winning the headman of each village to Christ opened entire areas to the gospel, as families tended to follow a headman's example.

All this time Father Wood was growing spiritually, though he occasionally slipped and smoked opium when he was having arthritic pain in the worst of the rainy season. Headman Honey forbade the other families at Ta-Ngo to become Christians, so Father Wood was often lonely.

"It isn't much fun being a Christian," he said one day to Belle.

Christmas time was near and the missionaries outdid themselves to make it a happy, family time, especially for Father Wood, including him in their festivities. They taught the Lisu American-style games, and soon Father Wood was absorbed in seeing how many times he could light a candle with a match, while dignified Headman Honey and Wu-be attempted to eat bananas hanging from a pole. The children ran three-legged races and dangled cardboard frogs on a string.

The villagers adjourned to Father Wood's shanty to see the Christmas story on a flannelboard. Father Wood surprised everyone by reading the Christmas story from Luke. From then on, he never complained—he had discovered Christian fellowship.

Four days later he woke with bad pain in his abdomen and told his wife he was "going home to God." He warned her against sacrificing a pig, or putting a silver coin in his mouth to pay for his entry into the next world. According to his premonition, he died, and went suddenly.

The unbelievers would not touch his body nor build a coffin nor dig a grave. Fearful of demon reprisal, they ordered the remaining Wood family to get out of the village. Wu-be dug the grave and wrapped his father's remains in an old mat. The villagers next attempted to starve the family.

Edna and Eileen, the two missionaries, had left Ta-Ngo, and while they were gone plunderers stole their personal possessions from Higgledy-Piggledy, the villagers all scattered, and Ta-Ngo was ploughed over as though it had never existed.

Though Father Wood could not walk enough to go out

and witness, he had spoken to everyone who passed his door, with not one soul being won. His voice lived on, however, for it was captured on a record by Gospel Recordings and was played in many villages all over North Thailand. On this disc Father Wood urged sinners to repent.

By 1955, the CIM-OMF was evangelizing eight tribes, three of whom needed their language put into writing: Lisu, Lahu, Yao, Blue Miao, White Miao, Shan, Pwo Karen, and Akha. The tribal churches became self-supporting, self-propagating and self-governing.

The Lisu tribe, in turn, reached out and evangelized the Lidi tribe, the Atsi-Kachin, the Wild Wa and the Tame Wa, the Jing-phaw, Shan and Nosu.

Before Mark of Goo-moo died, he had learned the Maru Kachin language and had seen one thousand tribesmen accept Christ.

"Now unto him that is able
to keep you
from falling,
and to present you faultless
before the presence
of his glory
with
exceeding
joy."
—Jude 24, one of Belle's favorite verses

XV

FAULTLESS . . . WITH JOY

On Belle's first field trip into North Thailand she had fallen twice and injured her chest. X-rays were negative, but a year later a lump was discovered. Belle underwent surgery in Chingmai, then was flown to New York and Philadelphia for further treatment, arriving November 14, 1954. She enjoyed the time spent in Wheaton, Illinois, with eleven-year-old Danny and Kathryn who was an accepted candidate of CIM-OMF. Another operation gave her the strength to finish her 8th book.

She passed into His presence March 20, 1957, her husband by her side. He remembered the light-hearted words spoken earlier:

"When I get to Heaven they aren't going to see much of me but my heels, for I'll be hanging over the golden wall keeping an eye on the Lisu Church!"